McMaster Journal of Theology and Ministry ISSN 1481-0794
ISBN 978-1-6667-0424

Editor
David J. Fuller

McMaster Divinity College
1280 Main Street West
Hamilton, Ontario, Canada L8S 4K1
email: mjtm@mcmaster.ca

McMaster Journal of Theology and Ministry is an electronic and print journal of McMaster Divinity College, in Hamilton, Ontario, Canada. It seeks to provide pastors, educators, and interested lay persons with the fruits of theological, biblical, and professional studies in an accessible form. It succeeds the Divinity College's former periodicals, the *Theological Bulletin*, *Theodolite*, and the *McMaster Journal of Theology*. Each volume covers an academic year (September to August). Reviews and articles are posted on the *MJTM* website at:

https://www.mcmaster.ca/mjtm/

and beginning with Volume Nine (2007–2008), the volume is available in hard copy as well.

The *McMaster Journal of Theology and Ministry* is also available on the EBSCO database, and abstracts are included in Religious and Theological Abstracts (RTA).

Manuscripts, books for review, and communications should be addressed to the Editor through the email address on the journal website. Contributors are encouraged to use the style of McMaster Divinity College, available at:

https://mcmasterdivinity.ca/resources-forms/mdc-style-guide/

All articles and book reviews are peer-reviewed for appropriate academic and professional standards. Special thanks to D. S. Martin for selecting and editing the poetry.

Copies of the printed version can be ordered from Wipf and Stock Publishers in Eugene, Oregon, USA, 97401, through their website, wipfandstock.com. Copies are also available through the McMaster Divinity College bookshop.

Content of the *McMaster Journal of Theology and Ministry* is copyright by McMaster Divinity College.

For more information about McMaster Divinity College, please visit the College's website at www.mcmasterdivinity.ca.

Back cover artwork: "The Heavens Declare, the Skies Proclaim," by Angela Lillico.

Artist's description: The fluid acrylic and mixed media painting, "The Heavens Declare, the Skies Proclaim," was conceived with a swirling design in mind. Blues and greens, darks and lights were chosen to support the idea of a heavenly sky. I have been using fluid acrylics for a number of years, striving to capture moments in time. In order for marbling to happen, the paint must be applied and manipulated while wet. This makes the process difficult to control because of the rapid drying time of acrylic, so speed is of the essence. I was thinking about Ps 19 as I was moving the paint around, feeling the excitement in the painting process and wondering how the Creator Himself felt when He actually formed the heavens. I also remembered the vision God had given Abram. He used the heavens to get His message across, and Scripture says He still uses the heavenly display to speak to us, no matter where we live. It is my desire that the viewer comes away with a sense of wonder, hope, and peace.

Artist's website: www.angelalillico.com.

BAUDELAIRE: INTRODUCTION AND PROSE POEMS

Burl Horniachek
Winnipeg, MB, Canada

XXIX: THE GENEROUS GAMBLER

Charles Baudelaire
Translated from French by Burl Horniachek and Ian McMillan
Winnipeg, MB, Canada and Edmonton, AB, Canada

Yesterday, through the crowd of the boulevard, I felt myself grazed by a mysterious Being whom I had always desired to know, and whom I recognized at once, though I had never seen him. There was undoubtedly an analogous desire relative to me within him, for he gave me, in passing, a significant wink of the eye, which I hastened to obey. I followed him attentively, and soon I descended behind him into a subterranean dwelling, dazzling, from which burst a luxury of which none of the superior habitations of Paris could provide an example anywhere close. It seemed strange to me that I had been able to pass so often alongside this prestigious lair without guessing its entrance. There reigned an exquisite, though heady, atmosphere, which made one forget almost instantly all the tedious horrors of life; there one breathed a dark bliss, analogous to that which was felt by the lotus-eaters when, landing on an enchanted island, illuminated by the gleams of an eternal afternoon, they felt born within them, with the drowsiness of the melodious cascades, the desire never to see again their penates, their wives, their children, and to never go back on the tall billows of the sea.

There were strange faces of men and women, marked with a fatal beauty, which it seemed I had already seen in eras and in countries which it was impossible for me to remember exactly, and who inspired in me a fraternal sympathy rather than that fear which ordinarily springs from the appearance of the unknown. If I wanted to try and define in any way the singular expression of their gaze, I would say that I never saw eyes shining more energetically with the horror of boredom and with the immortal desire to feel themselves alive.

My host and I were already, in sitting down, old and perfect friends. We ate, we drank immoderately all sorts of extraordinary wines, and, something no less extraordinary, it seemed to me that, after several hours, I was no more drunk than he. However, gambling, that superhuman pleasure, had cut off our frequent libations at various intervals, and I must say that I had played and lost my soul, in part bound, with heroic heedlessness and levity. The soul is a thing so impalpable, so often useless and sometimes so embarrassing, that I felt, with regard to this loss, only a little less emotion than if, on a walk, I had misplaced my calling card.

We smoked for a long time some cigars whose incomparable flavor and perfume gave the soul a longing for unknown countries and unknown happiness, and, intoxicated with all these delights, I dared, in an outburst of familiarity which did not seem to displease him, to cry out, grabbing hold of a cup full to the brim: "To your immortal health, you old goat!"

We also talked of the universe, of its creation and of its future destruction; of the great idea of the age, that is to say, of progress and perfectibility, and, in general, of all forms of human infatuation. On this subject, His Highness never ran out of light and irrefutable jokes, and he expressed himself with a smoothness of diction and a calmness in humour which I have not found in any of the most famous talkers of humanity. He explained to me the absurdity of the different philosophies which up to now had taken possession of the human brain, and even deigned to confide in me some fundamental principles of which it does not suit me to share the profit and possession with anyone . . . He did not complain in any way of the bad reputation he enjoyed in all parts of the world, assured me that he himself was the person most interested in the destruction of superstition, and swore to me that he had only ever been afraid, relative to his own power, one single time, it was the day he heard a preacher, more subtle than his colleagues, cry out in the pulpit: "My dear brethren, never forget, when you hear the progress of the Enlightenment extolled, that the devil's finest trick is to persuade you he does not exist!" The memory of that famous orator led us naturally to the subject of the academies, and my strange company affirmed to me that he did not disdain, in many cases, to inspire the pen, the word and the conscience of pedagogues, and that he was almost always present in person, though invisible, at all academic sessions.

Encouraged by so much kindness, I asked him for news of God, and if he had seen him recently. He replied, with a heedlessness shaded with a certain sadness: "We greet each other when we meet, but as two old gentlemen in whom an innate politeness cannot completely extinguish the memory of old grudges."

It is doubtful that His Highness had ever given such a long audience to a mere mortal, and I was afraid of taking advantage. Finally, as the shivering dawn whitened the windowpanes, this celebrated character, sung by so many poets and served by so many philosophers who work for his glory without knowing it, said: "I want you to keep a good memory of me, and to prove to you that I, of whom so much evil is said, am sometimes a *good devil*, to use one of your vulgar locutions. In order to make up for the irremediable loss you have made of your soul, I give to you the stake you would have won if fate had been on your side, that is to say the possibility of relieving and conquering, throughout your life, that strange affection of boredom, which is the source of all your diseases and all your miserable progress. Never will you form a desire without me helping you realize it; you will reign over your vulgar peers; you will be supplied with flattery and even adoration; silver, gold, diamonds, fairy palaces, will come seek you out and beg you to accept them, without your having made an effort to win them; you will change region and fatherland as often as your fancy dictates; you will gorge yourself on voluptuous pleasure, without fatigue, in charming lands where it is always warm and where the women smell as good as flowers—and so on, and so on . . . " he added, getting up and dismissing me with a good-natured smile.

If it had not been for the fear of humiliating myself before such a large assembly, I would have fallen willingly at the feet of this generous gambler, to thank him for his unprecedented munificence. But little by little, after I had left him, incurable distrust returned to my bosom; I no longer dared believe in so prodigious a happiness, and, as I was going to bed, still saying my prayers through a residue of idiotic habit, I repeated while half-asleep: "My God! Lord, my God! Make the devil keep his word!"

XLVII. Mademoiselle Bistoury

Charles Baudelaire
Translated from French by Burl Horniachek and Ian McMillan
Winnipeg, MB, Canada and Edmonton, AB, Canada

As I arrived at the far end of the suburb, under the flash of the gas lights, I felt an arm slip gently under mine, and I heard a voice that spoke in my ear: "Are you a doctor, sir?"

I looked; she was a tall, sturdy girl, with wide open eyes and lightly made up, her hair floating in the wind with the straps of her bonnet.

"No; I am not a doctor. Let me go."

"Oh yes! you are a doctor. I can see it well. Come to my place. You'll be very happy with me, come on!"

"No doubt, I will go and see you, but later, *after the doctor*, what the hell! . . . "

"Ah! ah!" she said, still hanging on my arm, and bursting with laughter, "you are a funny doctor; I have known many of that type. Come."

I passionately love mystery, because I always have the hope of untangling it. I let myself be carried off by that companion, or rather this unexpected enigma.

I omit the description of the hovel; you can find it in several well-known old French poets. Only, a detail unnoticed by Regnier, two or three portraits of famous doctors were hanging on the walls.

How I was pampered! Large fire, mulled wine, cigars; and, while offering me these good things, and lighting a cigar herself, the silly creature would say to me, "Make yourself at home, my friend, make yourself comfortable. It will remind you of the hospital and the good times of your youth.—Oh my! where did you get this white hair? You were not that way, not so long ago, when you were L's intern . . . I remember it was you who assisted him with the serious operations. Now there was a man who loved to cut, prune and trim! It was you who handed him the instruments, the threads and the sponges. And when, the operation done, he said proudly, looking at his watch: 'Five minutes, gentlemen!'—Oh! I get around. I know these gentlemen well."

A few moments later, addressing me with the familiar *tu*, she resumed her antiphon and said to me: "You're a doctor, aren't you, my kitten?"

This unintelligible refrain made me jump to my feet.

"No!" I shouted furiously.

"Surgeon, then?"

"No! no! unless it's to cut off your head! S . . . s . . . c . . . of s . . . m . . . !"

"Wait," she said, "you'll see."

And she drew from a cupboard a bundle of papers, which was nothing but a collection of portraits of the illustrious physicians of that time, lithographed by Maurin, which has been seen spread over the Quay Voltaire for several years.

"So! Do you recognize this one?"

"Yes! it is X. The name is at the bottom anyway; but I know him personally."

"I knew you did! Look! Here is Z, the one who said in his lecture, speaking of X. 'This monster who carries on his face the blackness of his soul!' All this because the other was not of his opinion in the same case! How we laughed at that in school, at the time! You remember it? Look, here is K., the one who denounced to the government the insurgents he treated at his hospital. It was the time of the riots. How is it possible that such a handsome man could have so little heart? Here now is W., a famous English physician; I caught him on his trip to Paris. He has the look of a young lady, does he not?"

And as I touched a bundle tied up, also laid on the pedestal table, "Wait just a bit," she said; "That's the interns, and this package is the externs."

And she spread out a mass of photographic images in a fan, representing much younger features.

"When we meet again, you will give me your portrait, won't you, my darling?"

"But," I said to her, following in my turn, me too, my obsession "Why do you believe I am a doctor?"

"Because you are so kind and good to women!"

"Strange logic!" I said to myself.

"Oh! I am hardly ever mistaken; I have known a good number. I love these gentlemen so much that, although I am not ill, I sometimes go see them for no other reason than to see them. There are some who tell me coldly: "You are not sick at all!" But there are others who understand me because I play a part for them."

"And when they do not understand you . . . ?"

"Great Mary! As I have bothered them *unnecessarily*, I leave ten francs on the mantel. They're so good and sweet, these men!—At Pitié Hospital I discovered a little intern, who is pretty as an angel, and who is polite! And who works hard, poor boy! His comrades told me he did not have money because his parents were poor and could not send him anything. It gave me confidence. After all, I'm a beautiful enough woman, though not so young. I said, 'Come see me, come see me often. And with me, do not worry; I do not need money.' But you understand that I let him know that in a host of ways; I did not tell him so crudely; I was so afraid of humiliating him, the dear child!—Well! would you believe that I have a funny desire that I dare not tell him?—I would like him to come and see me with his kit and apron, even with a little blood on it!"

She said that with an extremely candid look, as a sensitive man would say to an actress whom he loves: "I want to see you dressed in the costume you wore in that famous role you created."

As for me, I persisted, I continued: "Can you remember the time and occasion when this so particular passion was born within you?" With difficulty I made myself understood; finally I succeeded. But then she answered with a very sad look, and even, as far as I can remember, turning her eyes away: "I do not know... I do not remember."
What bizarre things can you not find in a big city, when you know to go about and look? Life teems with innocent monsters.—Lord my God! you, the Creator, you, the Master; you who have made Law and Freedom; you, the sovereign who lets be, the judge who pardons; you who are full of motives and causes, and who may have put in my mind this taste of horror to convert my heart, like healing at the end of a blade; Lord have mercy, have pity on madmen and fools! O Creator! Can there be monsters in the eyes of Him alone who knows why they exist, how they were made and how they might not have been made?

BAUDELAIRE AND CHRISTIANITY: AN INTRODUCTION

Burl Horniachek
Winnipeg, MB, Canada

NOTE: The following is intended as a supplement the above translations and to explain why readers of a theology journal might be interested in them and other works by Charles Baudelaire.

One might wonder why Christians in particular should be interested in a poet with such a reputation for Satanism and blasphemy, not to mention flagrant sexual immorality and conspicuous drug and alcohol abuse. Not only that, but his body of work often revels in the most disgusting imagery: spiders, whores, skeletons, vampires, worms, corpses, wounds, and disease. No wonder he has been detested and denounced by many Christians, both in his own lifetime and beyond. As Freeman Henry says:

The outcries of moral indecency, of irreverence, and of sacrilege followed swiftly the appearance of Les Fleurs du Mal in 1857 and culminated in the now-famous trial before the magistrates of Napoleon III's Sixth Correctional Chamber. The small fine and partial censure of the work (300 francs and six poems condemned) imposed by the court did not reflect, however, the outrage expressed by many religiously conservative readers. The friend and confessor of the poet's mother, abbe Cardinne, went so far as to burn the book, claiming it to be diabolical; and one of Baudelaire's staunchest supporters, Barbey d'Aurevilly, wrote that the poet of this strange volume of verse had but two options before him: either to commit suicide or to convert to Christianity.[1]

Nevertheless, Baudelaire's work has also found champions among many Christians, including writers such as François Mauriac, T. S. Eliot and Dana Gioia.[2] His poetry is suffused with Christian imagery, and frequently addresses serious theological issues. Furthermore, it should not be a surprise that Baudelaire eventually *did* have a sincere religious conversion to Catholic Christianity later in life, well before his death bed.[3] Still, the main body of his work, most of which was composed well before that conversion, does pose a challenge for many Christian readers.

Through the most of his adult life Baudelaire might fairly be described as Catholic without quite being Christian. While many who have defied Christian morality as he did in life have tended to an optimistic view of human nature, Baudelaire was not one of them. It is commonly said that, while Baudelaire did not believe

---

1. Henry, "Onomastics," 44. For a survey of the critical reactions to Baudelaire, positive and negative, up to 1917, see Carter, "Baudelaire devant la critique de 1857 à 1917." François Mauriac ("Charles Baudelaire the Catholic," 36) claimed that the priests who educated young men in France while he (Mauriac) was growing up excluded Baudelaire and Verlaine from their curriculum, even though they included secular authors such as Flaubert.
2. Eliot, "Baudelaire," 335–45; Gioia, "Conversation," 76, 79; Mauriac, "Charles Baudelaire the Catholic," 30–37.
3. The most substantial account of Baudelaire's conversion in English is in Enid Starkie's biography. See especially Starkie, *Baudelaire*, 530–34, 587–89, 608–9, 612. Baudelaire's religious poem "The Unforseen" was published 1863.

in any kind of redemption, he believed intensely in the reality of sin.[4] "To the Reader," the first poem in *Les Fleurs du Mal*, begins like this:

> Stupidity, delusion, selfishness and lust
> Torment our bodies and possess our minds
> While we sustain our affable remorse
> The way a beggar nourishes his lice.[5]

And the volume ends with this, from "Travelers":

> Chief among all the wonders we glimpsed,
> In every hole and corner, forced on our sight
> At every turn of fortune's fatal wheel—
> The boring pageant of immortal sin:
>
> Woman a slave and yet vainglorious,
> Stupid and unashamed in her self-love;
> Man a greedy tyrant, slave of his slaves,
> Swelling the sewer to stinking flood;
>
> Victims in tears, the hangman glorified
> The banquet seasoned and festooned with blood
> The poison of power clogs the despot's veins,
> And the people kiss the knout that scourges them.[6]

Baudelaire was a kind of hyper-Augustinian, seeing utter corruption and total depravity (in the theologically unsophisticated sense) in everything.[7] He saw nature and the whole created

---

4. See for example: "Baudelaire is not always certain in his notion of Good" (Eliot, "Baudelaire," 343); "All he had left at a certain point was to revel in his own damnation" (Gioia, "Conversation," 79); "It is frequently noted about Baudelaire that he sees sin but not redemption" (Meltzer, "Baudelaire, Maistre and Original Sin"). "Redemption, given this situation, appears hopeless" (Mills, "Charles Baudelaire," [n.p.]).
5. Baudelaire, *Les Fleurs du Mal*, 5; Baudelaire, *Oeuvres Complètes*, 1:5.
6. Baudelaire, *Les Fleurs du Mal*, 155; Baudelaire, *Oeuvres Complètes*, 1:132.
7. Meltzer, *Seeing Double*, 32. Meltzer, "Baudelaire, Maistre and Original Sin." As Meltzer says, Baudelaire's hyper-Augustinianism was egged on by his reading of Joseph de Maistre. However, Baudelaire's often rough treatment

world, and hence, by implication, its creator, as something fundamentally evil. As with many imaginative writers since the Enlightenment, his spirituality shares much with Gnosticism,[8] and indeed some of Baudelaire's speculations in prose do recall that ancient heresy:

> What is the fall?
> If it is unity become duality, it is God who has fallen.
> In other words, is not creation the fall of God?[9]

Accordingly, while Baudelaire was far from chaste in his personal life, he was no simple celebrant of sensual indulgence. For him, sex always has an inescapable moral component, however perverse. As he puts it in his notes:

> The unique and supreme pleasure of love lies in the absolute certainty of doing evil.[10]

There are certain layers of irony to that statement, but it seems clear that, for Baudelaire, as for many Gnostics, sexual reproduction was a horror and his work expresses a decided preference for non-reproductive sexual acts. In his novel, *La Fanfarlo*, the poet's alter ego is described thus:

> [H]e considered reproduction as a vice of love, pregnancy as a spider's malady. He had written somewhere: the angels are hermaphrodite and sterile.[11]

---

of God in his poetry was certainly not derived from Maistre. See also Leakey, *Baudelaire and Nature*, 140–41, 150–60. By no means was Baudelaire ever consistent in his condemnation of nature. As Leakey notes, even after Baudelaire began to adopt a more definite negative view of nature in 1852, his statements and poetic practice were always somewhat contradictory. Leakey, *Baudelaire and Nature*, 127–29, 134, 137, 317–20.

    8. There has been considerable controversy over the category of Gnosticism. See Brakke, "Imagining 'Gnosticism' and Early Christianities," 1–28 for a good discussion of the issue. I disagree with Brakke's ultimate conclusion and take Gnosticism to be a useful interpretive category. However, I agree that it was not a single unitary religion, either in ancient times or across history.

    9. Baudelaire, *Oeuvres Complètes*, 1:688
   10. Baudelaire, *Oeuvres Complètes*, 1:652
   11. Baudelaire, *Oeuvres Complètes*, 1:577

In the poem "Damned Women: Delphine and Hippollyta," Baudelaire goes on to commend lesbians for "the harsh sterility of [their] delight,"[12] while in the poem "Lesbos" he admires how the young women there "caress their ripened limbs in sterile joy."[13] Going against nature as they do, these relations cannot, of course, be free from suffering, but they do not perpetuate the painful existence of a sinful humanity, nor do they set the stage for the, at least for Baudelaire, necessarily horrifying struggle between mother and child. (His relationship with his mother was notoriously fraught.)

But, again, much like many with Gnostic tendencies, Baudelaire celebrates both abstinence *and* debauchery, exalting the far extremes of sexual practice, as here in "Damned Women":

> Virgins, demons, monsters, martyrs,
> All great spirits scornful of reality,
> Saints and satyrs in search of the infinite,
> Racked with sobs or loud with ecstasy.[14]

St. Anthony, nuns, lesbians, all get thrown into the hopper. All of them, in Baudelaire's view, seek a kind of pure transcendence that frustrates the ends of nature's god.

What most sets Baudelaire apart from the Gnostics, however, is that he does not expect any sort of salvation out of this. Gnosis cannot save, for the only possible knowledge is knowledge of one's doom. He does commend various methods for approaching the transcendent, but these things, sex, drugs, art, even virtue, offer only brief respites from a world fundamentally composed of suffering and despair. They may offer consolation, but no hope. In "Be Drunk" he says:

> So as not to be the martyred slaves of time, be perpetually drunk. On wine, on poetry, or on virtue, as you wish, but be drunk![15]

---

12. Baudelaire, *Les Fleurs du Mal*, 129. Baudelaire, *Oeuvres Complètes*, 1:155.
13. Baudelaire, *Les Fleurs du Mal*, 124. Baudelaire, *Oeuvres Complètes*, 1:150
14. Baudelaire, *Les Fleurs du Mal*, 130. Baudelaire, *Oeuvres Complètes*, 1:114.

However, just as his attitude towards sex is not one of uncomplicated celebration, Baudelaire was considerably more ambivalent about alcohol and drugs than his popular reputation might suggest. Drugs and alcohol likewise offer brief flashes of ecstasy, but they are still intimately connected with pain, and the temporary heaven they create is particularly empty and devoid of meaning. Baudelaire even devoted a large part to his book *Artificial Paradises* to the isolating dangers of hashish and the debilitations that come with opium, though he remained relatively positive towards wine.[16]

Above all, it is beauty which most lifts us most substantially out of the ordinary world. In "Hymn to Beauty," he writes:

> Angel or Siren, rhythm, fragrance, light,
> Provided you transform—O my one queen
> This hideous universe, this heavy hour.[17]

But, of course, even the experience of beauty fades. No matter how grand, complex or apparently complete the vision, one is forever being yanked back to reality, as in "The Double Room":

> [A]ll this magic dissolved at the brutal knock struck by the spectre... . Horrors! I remember! I remember! Yes! This hovel, this abode of eternal boredom, is truly mine. The furniture, stupid, dusty, chipped; the hearth without flame or coal, wet with spittle. The sad windows where the rain has traced its furrows in the dust; the manuscripts, effaced or incomplete; the almanac where pencil has marked off the unlucky dates.[18]

Furthermore, arising, as it so often does, out of the sexual appetite, beauty, the vision of the ideal, is forever tied to evil and the pain that attends it.

Just as he refuses to celebrate in any simple way the joys of sensual indulgence, Baudelaire kept some distance from what

---

15. Baudelaire, *Oeuvres Complètes*, 1:337.
16. Hemmings, "O Just, Subtle and Mighty Opium," 232–48. See also Burt, "Baudelaire and Intoxicants," 117–29.
17. Baudelaire, *Les Fleurs du Mal*, 29. Baudelaire, *Oeuvres Complètes*, 1:25.
18. Baudelaire, *Oeuvres Complètes*, 1:281.

might be called the alternative spiritualties of his era. He does make occasional references to the occult and obviously had at least some general familiarity with the subject, but the contrast with writers such as Honoré de Balzac, Victor Hugo, Robert Browning, or Butler Yeats is striking. *They* go on and on about their table-rappings and alchemical researches, sometimes writing whole books about them. But not only are references to alchemy and the occult in Baudelaire rather sparse, they tend towards the negative, as in "To the Reader":

> Satan Trismegistus subtly rocks
> Our ravished spirits on his wicked bed
> Until the precious metal of our will
> Is leached out by this cunning alchemist:[19]

It is true that the poet here revels in defeat and degradation, but it is defeat and degradation that he revels in. In "Alchemy of Suffering":

> Trismegistus intercedes:
> This ever-daunting guide
> Makes me a Midas in reverse,
> Saddest of alchemists–
>
> Gold turns to iron at my touch,
> Heaven darkens to hell;
> Clouds become a winding sheet[20]

However pessimistic about orthodox Christianity Baudelaire may be, he seems no less skeptical of any other routes to salvation.

Like many literary people in the nineteenth century, Baudelaire did show some interest in the eccentric Swedish visionary Emmanuel Swedenborg. It is unclear how much of Swedenborg

---

19. Baudelaire, *Les Fleurs du Mal*, 5; Baudelaire, *Oeuvres Complètes*, 1:5.
20. Baudelaire, *Les Fleurs du Mal*, 78; Baudelaire, *Oeuvres Complètes*, 1:77.

Baudelaire actually read,[21] but there are several brief references to the Swede in his work,[22] and he picked up on the Swedenborgian term "correspondences," which was used by Swedenborg to describe the intimate connection between the inner and outer, the material and spiritual worlds. Individual oddities aside, Swedenborg's system was largely a revival of medieval allegory[23] and his view of correspondences reflects a mostly conventional religious understanding of how the cosmos is structured: common things in the world point up to higher spiritual realities. Baudelaire adopted Swedenborg for his own purposes, often emphasizing more earthbound analogies, such as those between different kinds of sensual experiences (sounds, colours, textures) as well as those between the different arts (literature, music, painting),[24] but this does not mean Baudelaire had found anything especially heterodox in Swedenborgian correspondences themselves.

Despite his infernal reputation, direct references to Satan and other devils are relatively infrequent in Baudelaire. Perhaps this reputation exists because, when the devils do appear, they tend to be quite memorable. Satan himself first shows up in "To the Reader," audaciously conflated with the alchemical Hermes Trismegistus. Though hardly a pious poem, the portrait of Satan and the other devils there is not particularly objectionable from an orthodox perspective. They simply, though rather joyfully, preside over our sins:

> Wriggling in our brains like a million worms
> A demon demos holds its revels there,
> And when we breathe the Lethe in our lungs
> Trickles sighing on its secret course.[25]

---

21. Wilkinson, *The Dream of an Absolute Language*, 220–21; Starkie, *Baudelaire*, 261.
22. Wilkinson, *The Dream of an Absolute Language*, 219, 222–23.
23. Wilkinson, *The Dream of an Absolute Language*, 93, 97.
24. For discussions of Baudelaire's use of Swedenborg see Leakey, *Baudelaire and Nature*, 173–50; Starkie, *Baudelaire*, 260–69; Wilkinson, *The Dream of an Absolute Language*, 217–47.
25. Baudelaire, *Les Fleurs du Mal*, 5; Baudelaire, *Oeuvres Complètes*, 1:5.

In contrast, one of the most notorious poems, "The Litanies of Satan," offers up a direct prayer to Satan. He is presented as an exiled and wronged prince who sets himself up as patron of all "lepers and such outcast scum." He is:

> Adoptive father to those an angry God
> The Father drove from his earthly paradise.[26]

More ambivalently, in "Hymn to Beauty," Satan is portrayed as at least a potential source of beauty:

> Come from Satan, come from God—who cares[27]

Two of the prose poems also prominently feature devils. In "The Temptations, or Eros, Wealth and Fame," the temptations of the title are represented as three devils. Though all of them have a certain magnificence, the poet is not quite sold. As he says to Eros:

> [E]ven if I did not know you, old monster, your mysterious cutlery, your ambiguous vials, the chains in which your feet are entangled, are symbols which disclose quite clearly the disadvantages of your friendship. Keep your presents.[28]

There are similar words for the heavily tattooed Wealth:

> I have no need of the misery of any person for my enjoyment; and I do not want a richness saddened, like a wallpaper, with all the misfortunes represented on your skin.[29]

And Fame:

> I am not made to marry the mistress of certain people whom I do not care to name.[30]

In "The Generous Gambler," one of the prose poems presented above in a new translation, Satan himself appears. He is

26. Baudelaire, *Les Fleurs du Mal*, 143–44; Baudelaire, *Oeuvres Complètes*, 1:124–25.
27. Baudelaire, *Les Fleurs du Mal*, 29; Baudelaire, *Oeuvres Complètes*, 1:25.
28. Baudelaire, *Oeuvres Complètes*, 1:309.
29. Baudelaire, *Oeuvres Complètes*, 1:309.
30. Baudelaire, *Oeuvres Complètes*, 1:310.

presented as a witty and urbane nineteenth-century gentleman. The poet and the devil engage in some drinking and gambling, during which the poet rather carelessly loses his soul, and a droll discussion of the state of the world ensues. Then the devil makes some quite generous promises to make up for the poet's lost soul. Of course, the poet doesn't find the devil entirely trustworthy.

That is about it for Satan in the poems. However, together with the frequently macabre imagery, the often non-condemnatory depiction of sinful behaviour and the sometimes negative portrayal of God himself, the poems which do feature Satan begin to cast a shadow over the whole and can make it seem like that old serpent is actually the presiding spirit over all of them.

God himself in *Les Fleurs du Mal* is portrayed in multiple ambivalent and contradictory ways. In "To the Reader," the opening poem in *Les Fleurs du Mal*, God is simply absent. Elsewhere, as in "The Little Old Women," God can appear as the embodiment of a kind of impersonal fate:

> Ancient eves
> under God's undeviating paw[31]

In "Abel and Cain," God becomes a patron of the complacent middle class, apparently happy to see those on the margins ground into dust, thus becoming a worthy object of revolt:

> Race of Abel, sleep and feed,
> God is pleased.
>
> Grovel in the dirt and die,
> Race of Cain . . .
>
> Rise up, Race of Cain
> and cast God down upon earth![32]

---

31. Baudelaire, *Les Fleurs du Mal*, 97; Baudelaire, *Oeuvres Complètes*, 1:91.

32. Baudelaire, *Les Fleurs du Mal*, 142; Baudelaire, *Oeuvres Complètes*, 1:122–23.

In another poem, "St. Peter's Denial," God is even more straightforwardly wicked:

> Like a tyrant gorged on meat and wine, He sleeps
> The sound of our blasphemies sweet in His ears.
>
> The martyrs sobs, the screaming at the stake
> Compose, no doubt, a heady symphony;
> Indeed for all the blood their pleasure cost
> The heavens have not had half enough.[33]

Elsewhere, as in "The Litanies of Satan," God is portrayed as "jealous" and "angry." Yet, in contrast, the God of "Consecration," though still primarily a punisher of humans, at least aims to bring beauty, and thus a kind of *aesthetic* salvation, into being through that punishment:

> Thanks be to God who gives us suffering
> As sacred remedy for our sins,
> That best and purest element which prepares
> The strong in spirit for divine delights!
>
> I know the Poet has a place apart
> Among the holy legions blessed ranks;
> You will invite him to the eternal feast
> Of Dominations, Virtues, Thrones and Powers;
>
> I know that pain is the one nobility
> Upon which hell itself cannot encroach
> That if I am to weave my mystic crown
> I must braid into it all time, all space . . . [34]

Christ hardly appears in the poems. Aside from a few brief allusions, the most notable appearance is in "St. Peter's Denial." Jesus is generally portrayed quite positively there:

> And when they spat on your divinity,

---

33. Baudelaire, *Les Fleurs du Mal*, 141; Baudelaire, *Oeuvres Complètes*, 1:121.

34. Baudelaire, *Les Fleurs du Mal*, 12–13; Baudelaire, *Oeuvres Complètes*, 1:9.

> The jeering scullions and the conscript scum –
> That moment when you felt the thorns impale
> The skull which housed Humanity itself;[35]

But he is mainly used as foil for a monstrously wicked God the Father:

> Remember the Mount of Olives, Jesus? When
> You fell on your knees and prayed to Him
> Who laughed on high at the sound of hammering
> As the butchers drove the nails into your flesh?[36]

Ultimately, in a very Nietzschean move, the poet rejects the way of Jesus as weak and foolish:

> Myself, I shall be satisfied to quit
> A world where action is no kin to dreams;
> Would I had used—and perished—by the sword!
> Peter denied his master . . . He did well![37]

Theologically, the poem is in shambles, but it quite powerfully and coherently presents a certain mood.

Looking more generally at the pre-conversion body of Baudelaire's work, there is little consistency in his theology. Is evil good or is evil evil? Is God a tyrant to be defied or the source of goodness and beauty? Is Satan a source of energy for the artist and consolation for the outcast, or is he a false tempter? It is hard to know just what the poet thinks. For Baudelaire, there is definitely a top and a bottom, but one can never be sure exactly what goes where.[38] That might not be acceptable in a philosopher or systematic theologian, but for a poet as poet, it actually works well.

---

35. Baudelaire, *Les Fleurs du Mal*, 141–42; Baudelaire, *Oeuvres Complètes*, 1:121–22.
36. Baudelaire, *Les Fleurs du Mal*, 141–42; Baudelaire, *Oeuvres Complètes*, 1:121–22.
37. Baudelaire, *Les Fleurs du Mal*, 141–42; Baudelaire, *Oeuvres Complètes*, 1:121–22.
38. Meltzer ("Baudelaire, Maistre and Original Sin") states, "The concept of evil in Baudelaire frequently ends up sublating his radical binary structures, such that Satan and God are often conflated."

Enduring, as he did, poverty, illness, and neglect in the years after *Les Fleurs du Mal*, Baudelaire did eventually begin to turn sincerely to God. In a series of notes he begins to write:

- Prayer: charity, wisdom and strength.
- Without charity, I am only a resounding cymbal.
  My humiliations have been graces from God.
- My egotistical phase, is it over?[39]

A new humility appears in the poet. He no longer puts such value on worldly fame and success and he begins to pray with real devotion. He resolves:

> To pray every morning to God, the source of all power and all justice; to my father, to Mariette and to Poe, as intercessors; that they may give me the strength necessary to fulfil all my duties and that they may grant my mother a long enough life to enjoy my transformation; to work all day, or at least as long as my strength allows; to put my trust in God, that is to say, in Justice itself, for the success of my plans; to offer, every evening, a further prayer, asking God for life and strength for my mother and myself; to divide all my earnings into four parts—one for current expenses, one for my creditors, one for my friends and one for my mother —to obey the strictest principles of sobriety, the first of which is abstinence from all stimulants, whatever they may be.[40]

If "The Generous Gambler" is to be believed, Baudelaire had never completely ceased to pray:

> [A]s I was going to bed, still saying my prayers through a residue of idiotic habit, I repeated [my prayer] while half-asleep.[41]

But now he truly meant it. Baudelaire's faith was still a bit eccentric, featuring Edgar Allen Poe, along with his father and

---

39. Baudelaire, *Oeuvres Complètes*, 1:671.
40. Baudelaire, *Oeuvres Complètes*, 1:673.
41. Baudelaire, *Oeuvres Complètes*, 1:328, 1154–55, 1336–37. Baudelaire likely had started "The Generous Gambler" by 1860. It was completed and published by 1864. We can't say for sure which was finished first, but his religious poem "The Unforseen" was published in 1863, before "The Generous Gambler."

childhood nurse, as interceding saints, but it was sincere for all that.

There are still not many references to Christ, though there is this intriguing late fragment:

> The dynamic ethic of Jesus. Renan finds it ridiculous that Jesus should believe in the omnipotence, even over matter, of prayer and faith. The sacraments are the means of this dynamic.[42]

And in the notes for his never completed book on Belgium, he does write of how moved he was at the sight of "the eternal crucified" lifted up in procession.[43] It is apparent that Baudelaire's faith was Catholic and Christian, rather than merely a general belief in God.

Though Baudelaire's turn to religion is clear from his unfinished notes, it does not much appear in his finished literary works. There are a few prayers in the pre-conversion work, such as in the lines from "Consecration" quoted above, but they can come off as a bit self-aggrandizing or even selfish. Here is the ending of "One O'Clock in the Morning":

> Souls of those I have loved, souls of those I have sung, give me strength, sustain me, banish from me the lies and corrupting vapours of the world. And you, oh Lord my God! grant me the grace to write a few fine poems, so that I may know that I am not the least of men, that I am not inferior to those I despise.[44]

There is what appears to be a more sincere prayer at the end of "A Voyage to Cythera," where the poet, beholding an image of himself crucified by lust, cries out:

> Lord, give the strength and courage to behold
> My body and my heart without disgust.[45]

---

42. Baudelaire, *Oeuvres Complètes*, 1:706.
43. Baudelaire, *Oeuvres Complètes*, 2:942.
44. Baudelaire, *Oeuvres Complètes*, 1:288.
45. Baudelaire, *Les Fleurs du Mal*, 136; Baudelaire, *Oeuvres Complètes*, 1:119.

But the most notable sincere prayer in the finished works is in "Mademoiselle Bistoury," the other prose poem presented here in a new translation.[46] The poet encounters a mentally ill woman with a fetish for surgeons. She invites him up to her apartment and tries to convince him that he is a surgeon, so she can begin a romantic relationship with him. The poet admirably refuses to take advantage of her and then ends the poem with a plea to God for understanding of such a strange and disturbing occurrence. Much as in the Book of Job, the new "monsters" of the modern city provoke the narrator into a deep questioning of God, a questioning which, however, is not quite a rejection or indictment of him. Despite the young woman's terrifying illness, for which she is not guilty, God is still appealed to as the standard of good. As T. S. Eliot notes in his essay on Baudelaire: for there really to be a down implies there really is an up.[47] Encounters with sin as sin, or with degradation as degradation, can often, surprisingly, point us upward to God.

At this point, Baudelaire had begun to take the Devil more seriously too. In the earlier "The Generous Gambler" the irony is so layered so thick that it is difficult to know just how seriously he took pronouncements like this:

> My dear brethren, never forget, when you hear the progress of the Enlightenment extolled, that the devil's finest trick is to persuade you he does not exist![48]

Though I suspect even then he took it more seriously than many suppose, by the time of his verse poem "The Unforseen," there is no doubt:

> Whereupon appears One they had all denied—

Crucially, however, Baudelaire now thinks there is some true escape from all this sin and evil:

---

46. "Mademoiselle Bistoury" is almost certainly a post-conversion work. Baudelaire only submitted it for periodical publication in 1867, the year of his death, and it was finally published posthumously in 1869 in book form, along with all of his other prose poems. Baudelaire, *Oeuvres Complètes*, 1:1347.
47. Eliot, "Baudelaire," 338–39, 343–44.
48. Baudelaire, *Oeuvres Complètes*, 1:327.

> My soul in Thy hands is more than a futile toy
> And thy wisdom is infinite[49]

His own concluding note says:

> Here the author of Les Fleurs du Mal is turning towards eternal life. It had to end up this way.[50]

Baudelaire's health did not permit much time to see how his newfound faith would manifest itself in art, but even the earlier work has value for the theologically minded. Something like "The Generous Gambler" is not all that far off from C. S. Lewis' *The Screwtape Letters*, which it might have influenced. (Lewis refers to Baudelaire a couple times and must have read at least some of his work.)[51] Indeed, the quote about the devil's finest trick has often been attributed to Lewis himself. Negative images of the world can still reveal God, and Baudelaire at his most perverse was never in denial about the terrible corruptness of human desire. Thus his work has the constant bite of reality to it.

Bibliography

Baudelaire, Charles. *Les Fleurs du Mal*. Translated by Richard Howard. Jaffrey, NH: David R. Godine, 1982.

———. *Oeuvres Complètes*, edited by Claude Pichois. 2 vols. Paris: Gallimard, 1975–1976.

Brakke, David. "Imagining 'Gnosticism' and Early Christianities." In *The Gnostics: Myth, Ritual, and Diversity in Early Christianity*, 1–28. Cambridge, MA: Harvard University Press, 2011.

---

49. Baudelaire, *Oeuvres Complètes*, 1:171–72. We cannot say whether "The Unforseen" or "The Generous Gambler" was completed first.
50. Baudelaire, *Oeuvres Complètes*, 1:171.
51. Lewis, *The Pilgrim's Regress*, 208; Lewis, "C. S. Lewis to E. R. Eddison, January 19, 1943," 546.

Burt, E. S. "Baudelaire and Intoxicants" In *The Cambridge Companion to Baudelaire*, edited by Rosmary Lloyd, 117–29. Cambridge: Cambridge University Press, 2005.

Carter, A.E. "Baudelaire devant la critique de 1857 à 1917." MA diss., McGill University, 1942.

Eliot, T. S. "Baudelaire" In *Selected Essays*, 335–45. New York: Harcourt, Brace & Co., 1932.

Gioia, Dana. "A Conversation with Dana Gioia." Interview by Erika Koss. *Image* 73 (2012) 65–80.

Hemmings, F. W. J. "O Just, Subtle and Mighty Opium" In *Baudelaire the Damned*, 232–48. London: Bloomsbury, 1982.

Henry, Freeman G. "Onomastics and Religion in Baudelaire's Les Fleurs du Mal," *Literary Onomastics Studies* 10 (1983) 43–54.

Leakey, F. W. *Baudelaire and Nature*. Manchester: University of Manchester Press, 1969.

Lewis, C. S. *The Pilgrim's Regress*. Grand Rapids: Eerdmans, 2014.

———. "C. S. Lewis to E. R. Eddison, January 19, 1943." In *The Collected Letters of C. S. Lewis, Volume II: Books, Broadcasts and War, 1931–1949*, edited by Walter Hooper, 546. New York: HarperOne, 2004.

Mauriac, François. "Charles Baudelaire the Catholic." In *Baudelaire: A Collection of Critical Essays*, edited by Henri Peyre, 30–37. Translated by Lois A. Haegert. Englewood Cliffs, NJ: Prentice Hall, 1962.

Meltzer, Françoise. "Baudelaire, Maistre and Original Sin," *Church Life Journal*, April 9, 2019. https://churchlifejournal.nd.edu/articles/baudelaire-maistre-and-original-sin.

———. *Seeing Double: Baudelaire's Modernity*. Chicago: University of Chicago Press, 2011.

Mills, Kathryn Oliver. "Charles Baudelaire," Poetry Foundation, [n.d.], https://www.poetryfoundation.org/poets/charles-baudelaire.

Starkie, Enid. *Baudelaire*. London: Faber & Faber, 1957. Reprint, London: Penguin, 1971.

Wilkinson, Lynn R. *The Dream of an Absolute Language: Emmanuel Swedenborg and French Literary Tradition*. Albany: State University of New York Press, 1996.

God Our Suffering Mother? Kenotic Atonement in Julian of Norwich's Revelations of Divine Love

Matthew D. Burkholder
Wycliffe College, Toronto, ON, Canada

Introduction

Suffering is perhaps the greatest challenge to belief in the Christian God. For many, suffering is experienced in silence, leading to much secret pondering about how it can be that a loving God allows his creation to experience pain. Some wonder aloud, challenging God or defending him, trying to make sense of something universally experienced. It is therefore surprising when suffering is requested, just as it was by Mother Julian of Norwich in the fourteenth century. Julian, an anchorite and the earliest known female English writer, produced a work detailing her theology and experiences known as *Revelations of Divine Love*. This article examines the historical context of Julian's life and her theology of sin and argues that her theology of the Motherhood of God strengthens a kenotic understanding of Christ's atonement.[1]

---

1. Kenosis refers to the theology of Christ's self-emptying love based on the Apostle Paul's words in Phil 2:6–8: "Who, though he was in the form of God, did not regard equality with God as something to be exploited, but emptied himself, taking the form of a slave, being born in human likeness. And, being found in human form, he humbled himself and became obedient to the point of death—even death on a cross" (NRSV).

Biography

Modern historians know very few details regarding Julian of Norwich's life.[2] What is known directly of Julian's life experiences comes by way of what she shares in her only known work, *Revelations of Divine Love*. Julian's writings have survived in two formats, the "Short-Text" (ST), which includes initial reactions to a series of visions Julian experienced on what was perceived to be her death bed, and the "Long-Text" (LT), a subsequent work written fifteen to twenty years later which includes more profound reflections on her experience.[3] Julian's visions are delineated into sixteen "showings," or "special revelations," and are explained over eighty-six chapters in the LT.[4]

For Julian, the only details of her life worth sharing were those which furthered the purpose of espousing God's great love for humanity.[5] Any explicit personal details such as her family life, education, the context of her vocation as an anchorite, or even her given name, are absent in her writing.[6] The LT reflects her growing understanding that what she was shown was not for her alone, but the church as a whole. Thus, almost every usage of a personal pronoun when referring to the recipient of her vision in the ST was replaced by the plural "we."[7] Of importance for Julian is not her accomplishments, but "that our Lord God wishes us to have great regard for all the deeds he has done in the noble splendour of creating all things, and the excellence of man's creation (which is superior to all God's other works), and the

---

2. For more on the life of Julian, see Frykholm, *Julian*; Jantzen, *Julian of Norwich*; and Rolf, *An Explorer's Guide*.
3. Jantzen, *Julian of Norwich*, 15.
4. For a medieval edition of Julian's works, see Watson and Jenkins, eds., *The Writings of Julian*. For a modern English translation, see Julian, *Revelations*.
5. Jantzen, *Julian of Norwich*, 4.
6. The name "Julian" arises from the custom of an anchoress adopting the name of the church to which she was associated with, thus Julian most likely took her name from the Church of St. Julian, a church built during the reign of Cnut the Great at the beginning of the tenth century (Jantzen, *Julian of Norwich*, 4).
7. Turner, *Julian*, 73.

precious atonement which he has made for man's sin, turning all our blame into everlasting glory."[8] For Julian, this accomplishment trumps anything she could say about herself.

There are some biographical details, however, which emerge when analyzing Julian's writing. She dates her vision as occurring on 8 May 1373, when she was roughly "thirty and a half years old."[9] Based on this date Julian was born roughly in December of 1342. Julian was known to be "still alive in the year of our Lord 1413" and is thought to have died sometime after 1416.[10] Julian is described as an anchorite (recluse) within *Revelations*, which is confirmed in four surviving wills dating between 1393/94 and 1416.[11] Some believe that before becoming an anchorite, Julian was a Benedictine nun who served at a convent in Carrow located a mile outside of Norwich.[12] Her response at the beginning of her revelation, "Benedicite dominus!" was a typical greeting formula used between Benedictine monks and nuns, and Christ thanked Julian in her vision for her service "in her youth," as though she had consecrated herself for Christian service.[13]

Although Julian is described as "one who could not read,"[14] the sophistication she shows in understanding the implications of the theological concepts of late medieval theology suggests that she received a formal study of language.[15] The conflict between the sophisticated Julian and the self-described "unlettered" Julian

---

8. Julian, *Revelations*, 40.
9. Julian, *Revelations*, 4.
10. The Editors of Encyclopaedia Britannica, "Julian of Norwich," [n.p.].
11. Roger Reed, rector of St. Michael's, Coslany, Norwich donated to her two shilling when he died in 1393/94 and Thomas Emund, a chantry priest in Aylesham, Norfolk, gave twelve pence in 1404/05 as well as eight pence to a certain "Sarah, living with her." John Plumpton, a Norfolk merchant, gave 40 pence in 1414 to "the anchoress in the church of St. Julian's." Finally, Isabel Ufford, an aristocratic nun at the great house of Campsey in Suffolk gave the sum of twenty shillings to Julian in 1416 (Watson and Jenkins, eds., *The Writings of Julian*, 5).
12. Watson and Jenkins, eds., *The Writings of Julian*, 4.
13. Watson and Jenkins, eds., *The Writings of Julian*, 4.
14. Julian, *Revelations*, 39.
15. Watson and Jenkins, eds., *The Writings of Julian*, 10.

remains an enigma.[16] It may be possible that Julian lacked a robust education in Latin.[17] Norwich, however, had great libraries as the Benedictine Monks had homes and centers just across from the Julian church, of which Julian perhaps availed herself.[18] Nonetheless, the common and lowly English language, which Julian spoke, served as the perfect medium for someone seeking a humble life of service.[19]

Perhaps the most significant event of Julian's young life in Norwich was the arrival of the Black Death in the spring of 1349, which decimated a population of approximately thirteen thousand people in a vibrant economic center to half that number.[20] By the age of six or seven, Julian would have witnessed an unbelievable amount of death. The plague, which first devastated China, Central Asia, and the Middle East by killing approximately twenty-five million people from 1332–1357, set sail in October 1347 from the Black Sea port of Caffa aboard a cargo ship and landed in Messina, Italy, sweeping itself through Italy and making its way throughout Europe.[21] The Church, which lost approximately half of all its clergy during this period, struggled to minister to the dying who feared eternal damnation.[22] One must wonder when Julian asked for "three gifts of grace by God," including the experience of severe bodily sickness, if she held the horrific images of the Black Death in her mind as a reference point for her request.[23]

The exact context of how the Black Death affected Julian is not surprisingly a matter of speculation. How much of her family survived?[24] Did she marry and did she have children? Did she

16. Watson and Jenkins, eds., *The Writings of Julian*, 10.
17. Jantzen, *Julian of Norwich*, 16.
18. Jantzen, *Julian of Norwich*, 19.
19. Frykholm, *Julian*, 12.
20. Rolf, *An Explorer's Guide*, 28.
21. Rolf, *An Explorer's Guide*, 25.
22. Rolf, *An Explorer's Guide*, 30.
23. Julian, *Revelations*, 40.
24. One member of Julian's family that survived the Black Death was her mother, who was present during Julian's sickness and vision. See Julian, *Revelations*, 15.

lose children in the Black Death? Was she a widow? Perhaps Julian's unique approach to Trinitarian theology in which she intimately describes Jesus as "mother" in chapter 58 of the LT suggests first-hand experiential knowledge of parenthood?[25] Nonetheless, the details of Julian's life seem destined to remain in a type of "reputation-limbo," and continue to serve as an obstacle for her full canonization into sainthood by the Roman Catholic church.[26] In addition to such a devastating epidemic, Julian also experienced an "ugly age" of dislocation and confusion for the church as an adult.[27] Whether it be the Hundred Years War between England and France (1338–1453), the anxiety surrounding Lollardy and the "heretic" John Wycliffe, or the division of the Great Western Schism, Julian lived in remarkably tumultuous times.[28]

From Shame to Honor

This bleak biographical context, however limited, stands in direct contrast to Julian's hopeful outlook. One of the remarkable aspects of Julian's writing is that she did not share in the prevailing view that God had sent the plague as an act of judgement for sin, nor the atonement as an event which placated the wrath of a vindictive God.[29] Although Julian believes that "wickedness has been allowed to rise up in opposition to goodness," this wickedness is met by a God who, "opposed wickedness and turned everything to goodness and to glory for all those who shall be saved; for that is the quality in God which does good against evil."[30] According to Julian, one has little trouble believing in a God of punishment but struggles to accept a God that loves humanity tenderly.[31] As one Julian researcher notes: "Julian shrewdly penetrates into the strange inability of human nature to accept the

25. Julian, *Revelations*, 127.
26. Law, "In the Centre," 183.
27. Cooper, *Julian*, 9.
28. Cooper, *Julian*, 118.
29. Dearborn, "The Crucified Christ," 289.
30. Julian, *Revelations*, 128.
31. Nuth, "Two Medieval Soteriologies," 636.

self as lovable, making us paradoxically more comfortable with God the judge, whom we must always strive to please and appease, than with God the mother, who simply loves us as we are."[32] For Julian, how could such love without wrath co-exist with the realities of sin, Satan, and even church tradition?[33] According to Julian, this question brought about an answer of profound hope:

> And, it seemed to me that if there had been no sin, we should all have been pure and like our Lord, as he made us; and so, in my folly, I had often wondered before this time why, through the great foreseeing wisdom of God, the beginning of sin was not prevented; for then, it seemed to me, all would have been well. I should have given up such thoughts, yet I grieved and sorrowed over this, unreasonably and without discretion. But Jesus, who in this vision informed me of everything needful to me, answered with these words and said, "*Sin is befitting, but all shall be well, and all shall be well, and all manner of things shall be well.*"[34]

Christ's power—both in his Incarnation and his Second Coming—is that of one who performs not an act of judgment, but of redemption, and all Julian can say is that she is confident that all manner of things shall be well.[35] In contemplating God in this mystery, "our use of our reason is now so blind, so base, so uninformed, that we cannot recognize the high, marvelous wisdom, the power, and the goodness of the blessed Trinity."[36] And even though Julian accepts the teaching of the church that "many will be damned," something she struggles to accept as consistent with all things being well, she hopefully believes that by God's "great deed," he will mysteriously bring about a salvation where "he will make well all that is not well."[37] *What* exactly this great

---

32. Nuth, "Two Medieval Soteriologies," 636.
33. Heath, "Judgement Without Wrath," 38.
34. Julian, *Revelations*, 74–75. Italics added.
35. Heath, "Judgement Without Wrath," 45.
36. Julian, *Revelations*, 79.
37. Julian, *Revelations*, 80.

deed will be and *how* Christ will accomplish it is veiled in mystery known to none "under Christ."[38]

Although not explicitly, Julian's enigmatic approach to soteriology challenges the scholastic theological methods that had begun to dominate her time. The Middle Ages signifies a dramatic shift away from the ransom theory of the atonement by way of two dominant medieval figures, Anselm of Canterbury and Peter Abelard. In Anselm's view, the ransom theory of the atonement created a double allegiance to both God and the devil and granted the former rights over humanity.[39] According to Anselm, the issue at hand is that God was robbed of his honor because of human disobedience and that Christ's death makes a necessary atoning satisfaction for sin. According to Abelard, since the devil used seduction and the false promise of eternal life to ensnare humanity, the idea of him receiving rights over humanity in their ensuing sin is deeply problematic.[40] Both Anselm and Abelard recognize that since humanity sins only against God, the idea of a ransom being paid to the devil accounts for nothing.[41] From there, however, Anselm and Abelard diverge in their understandings of the atonement. For Anselm, the Incarnation is that which allows both the object of sin (God) and the agent of sin (humanity) to make recompense for God's lost honor, an approach he outlines in his work *Cur Deus Homo*, or, *Why God Became Human*.[42] For Abelard, "the atonement was primarily an act of love that inspired love for him in humans."[43] In the words of Abelard:

> Now it seems to us that we have been justified by the blood of Christ and reconciled to God in this way: through this unique act of grace manifested to us—in that his Son has taken upon himself our nature and preserved therein in teaching us by word and example even unto death—he has more fully bound us to himself by love; with the result

---

38. Julian, *Revelations*, 81.
39. Walters, "The Atonement," 242.
40. Walters, "The Atonement," 242.
41. Walters, "The Atonement," 242.
42. Anselm, "Why God Became Man," 260–355.
43. Walters, "The Atonement," 245.

that our hearts should be enkindled by such a gift of divine grace, and true charity should not now shrink from enduring anything for him.[44]

These two theories, Anselm's satisfaction theory and Abelard's moral influence theory, were foundational for the ongoing medieval debate about the meaning of the life and death of Christ.

Where is Julian situated in this context? Unlike Anselm's investigation into the Incarnation in *Cur Deus Homo*, Julian is content to live in hopeful anticipation of future salvation without the need for a complete and reasonable explanation of why God became human. Like Anselm, Julian believes that Christ's suffering provides an adequate understanding of the central mysteries of Christianity and produces an intelligible answer for the Incarnation, but their theological methods differed significantly.[45] In *Cur Deus Homo*, Anselm hopes to produce a non-scriptural, rational argument for the Incarnation, while Julian focuses on her personal experience to take comfort in what can "cast out of her mind forever all fear of sin and damnation."[46] For Julian, the only clear answer for the Incarnation is the all-consuming love of God.[47] Should we force Julian into a category of an atonement theory, her focus on the all-consuming love of God shares the similar perspective of Abelard. Julian, however, conceives of the solution to sin in much more mystical terms. For Julian, Christian hope resides in an intense understanding of humanity's unity with Christ.

---

44. Quoted in Walters, "The Atonement," 245.
45. Nuth, "Two Medieval Soteriologies," 619.
46. Nuth, "Two Medieval Soteriologies," 620.
47. One of the ways Julian (*Revelations*, 45) perceives of this reality is through a vision of a little hazelnut: "And in this vision he also showed a little thing, the size of a hazelnut, lying in the palm of my hand, as it seemed to me, and it was round as a ball. I looked at it with my mind's eye and thought, 'What can this be?' And the answer came in a general way, like this, 'It is all that is made.' I wondered how it could last, for it seemed to me so small that it might have disintegrated suddenly into nothingness. And I was answered in my understanding, 'It lasts, and always will, because God loves it; and in the same way everything has its being through the love of God.'"

Julian's hope, however, while appearing to border on the naïve, is grounded not in a denial of the destructive capability of sin, but in examining sin while considering one's unity with Christ. The Incarnation reveals both that God considers humanity his noblest creation, and that "the supreme essence and the most exalted virtue is the blessed soul of Christ."[48] Unity, therefore, with Christ's beloved soul unites "with a knot so subtle and so strong that it is united to God," and that in this unity one is made endlessly holy without end."[49] With unity to Christ comes the great victory over sin. Accordingly, the battle between sin and love is radically unequal because sin is anticipated by love, and sin only attempts to find its meaning independently of what it attempts to deny—the love of God.[50] Sin, in this context, is "nothing," and a reflection of Augustine's understanding of sin as misdirected love.[51] Sin, however, was not merely that which affected the human will to love, but that which brought about a cost to God, namely God's isolation from his creation and participation in humanity's suffering.[52]

For Julian, God experiencing isolation and suffering produces a unique perspective on the Fall. Julian challenges a popular perception of human culpability in her version of the popular medieval Parable of the Lord and the Servant, a parable that Anselm describes in *Cur Deus Homo*:

> But if there is blame inherent in the incapacity itself, the incapacity does not mitigate the sin itself, any more than it excuses the person who does not repay the debt. For suppose someone assigns his bondslave a task, and tells him not to leap into a pit from which he cannot by any means climb out, and that bondslave, despising the command and advice of his master, leaps into the pit which has been pointed out to him, so that he is completely unable to carry out the task assigned to him. Do you think that his incapacity serves in the

---

48. Julian, *Revelations*, 119.
49. Julian, *Revelations*, 119.
50. Turner, *Julian*, 94.
51. Shea, *Medieval Women*, 142. For Augustine's theology of sin as misdirected love, see *City of God* 12.8.
52. Shea, *Medieval Women*, 143.

slightest as a valid excuse for him not to perform the task assigned to him?[53]

According to Anselm, the servant's decision to disobey his master is a direct result of his voluntary action, rendering him unable to carry out his duty to his master. The central problem for Anselm is that "there is nothing in the universal order more intolerable than that a creature should take away from the Creator the honor due to him, and not repay what he takes away."[54] In Anselm's theology, Christ's Incarnation and death restores humanity's debt of honor.[55]

Now consider Julian's version of the parable:

> So, for the first, I saw two persons in bodily likeness, that is to say, a lord and a servant; and with that God gave me spiritual understanding. The lord sits in solemn state, in rest and in peace; the servant stands by respectfully in front of his lord, ready to do his lord's will. The lord looks at his servant very lovingly and kindly, and he gently sends him to a certain place to do his will. The servant does not just walk but suddenly springs forward and runs in great haste to do his lord's will out of love. And at once he falls into a hollow and receives very severe injury. And then he groans and moans, and wails and writhes, but he cannot rise nor help himself in any way. And the greatest harm of all that I saw him in was a lack of comfort; for he could not turn his face to look at his loving Lord, who was very close to him and in whom is all comfort; but, like someone who was weak and foolish for the moment, he was intent on his own feelings and went on suffering in misery.[56]

---

53. Anselm, "Why God Became Man," 309–10.
54. Anselm, "Why God Became Man," 262.
55. Anselm ("Why God Became Man," 349) notes that "No member of the human race except Christ ever gave to God, by dying, anything which that person was not at some time going to lose as a matter of necessity. Nor did anyone ever pay a debt to God which he did not owe. But Christ of his own accord gave to his Father what he was never going to lose as a matter of necessity, and he paid, on behalf of sinners, a debt which he did not owe."
56. Julian, *Revelations*, 106–7.

One notices significant differences between the two parables.[57] In Anselm's parable, the servant is fundamentally responsible for his fall, while in Julian's, the servant is eager to carry out his task and, in his haste, and out of love, he falls. For Julian, that humans sin and are deserving of punishment is not a complete truth but a necessary function to a greater truth: God will reward humanity if the knowledge of sin leads to contrition and penance which, in turn, allows God to respond with mercy and grace.[58] The remarkable suffering for Julian is that the servant appears to be utterly alone in his fallen state, but is only unaware that his lord can still see him.[59] Julian, who says it took "three months short of twenty years after the time of the revelation"[60] to understand the parable concludes that "only suffering blames and punishes, and our courteous Lord comforts and succors; he is always gladly regarding the soul, loving and longing to bring us bliss."[61] Instead of blame and punishment, God views the servant with a double aspect—"one outward, most gently and kindly, with great compassion and pity, and this was the first aspect; the other was inward, more spiritual, and this was revealed through my understanding being led into the lord, when I saw him greatly rejoicing over the honourable restoring and nobility

---

57. Although the parable is medieval in origin, Thomas Bennett ("Julian of Norwich," 315) has noted several ways how the parable resembles biblical imagery: "In almost every way, Julian's parable is fashioned from imagery derived from the Gospels. The central characters are a lord and his servant, a common Gospel trope (e.g. Matt 18:21–35; 25:14–30). As in the biblical master-servant parables, the servant has a commission to be a laborer in the fields, thus paralleling a number of Jesus' parables concerning farms and vineyards. The servant is injured, in need of rescue, which may echo the parable of the lost sheep (Matt 18:12–14; Luke 15:3–7). Moreover, Julian explains the parable using what Sutherland deems 'the conventional tools of biblical interpretation.' That is, Julian first shares the parable, then she proceeds to explain its symbolism. This should remind us of, for example, the parable of the sower (Matt 13:1–23; Mark 4:1–20; Luke 8:4–15)."
58. Healy-Varley, "Wounds Shall be Worships," 194.
59. Heath, "Judgement Without Wrath," 39.
60. Julian, *Revelations*, 108.
61. Julian, *Revelations*, 109.

to which he would and must bring his servant through his abundant grace."[62]

The theological implications of Julian's parable were a source of anxiety for her. In chapter 50 of the LT, which precedes the Parable of the Lord and the Servant, Julian admits her struggle to reconcile the God who does not "blame us in any way" with the "common teaching of Holy Church" that "the blame for our sins weighs upon continually."[63] However, since human fallenness, according to Julian's vision, is bound up in Christ's own "fallenness," some of her tension is alleviated. Julian realizes that the servant represents both Christ and Adam and that when Adam fell, Christ fell in order to save Adam from hell.[64] Christ, who has taken upon himself for all time human fallenness, commits himself to an utter solidarity with humanity, experiencing crucifixion and death, then descending into hell to perform a mighty deed of salvation.[65] Julian's theology begins and ends with the infinite love of God, a love that transcends sin and permanently unites God and humanity.[66] As one Julian researcher notes: "While Julian never fully resolves the paradox of God's mercy and justice co-mingled, she interprets the mystery she does not understand in light of the truth she knows. God may be trusted with the unknown, because God is trustworthy with the known. God is love. This is the basis for everything else."[67]

The Adam/Christ typology that plays a significant role in Anselm's writing is based on an essential differentiation between Christ and humanity.[68] In Anselm's theology of the Incarnation, Christ is divine and innocent whereas humanity is guilty; alternatively, in Julian's theology there is almost no distinction.[69] Once again Julian finds herself dialoguing with the longstanding theological opinions of her era in a novel way. Unlike the

62. Julian, *Revelations*, 107.
63. Julian, *Revelations*, 105.
64. Nuth, *Wisdom's Daughter*, 30.
65. Heath, "Judgement Without Wrath," 41.
66. Heath, "Judgement Without Wrath," 41.
67. Heath, "Judgement Without Wrath," 41.
68. Nuth, "Two Medieval Soteriologies," 632.
69. Nuth, "Two Medieval Soteriologies," 632.

Augustinian tradition of seeing the ontological nature of the will as being in unified opposition to God and others, Julian differentiates between an "upper will" and "lower will," with the higher will never having assented to sin.[70] Echoing Augustine's notion of sin as misguided love, Julian agrees that "all our difficulty is because of a failure of love on our part," but the lack of wrath and judgement she observes in her vision forces her to define the will in a sense more congruent to her developing theology of sin.

David Aers, in his book *Salvation and Sin*, notes that Julian's theology of the unfallen will had already emerged as a point of criticism by Augustine in his book *Confessions*. Augustine, who encountered the Manichees in Rome, recalls how their teaching allowed him to think of sin as resulting from an alien nature so that it was if he had done nothing wrong and remained "free of blame" when sinning.[71] Although it would be difficult to claim that Julian intended to produce this response to her definition of the unfallen will, Aers rightfully sees this theology as problematic.[72] By describing sin externally to a godly and untouched will, which is always united to God, "the sinner's 'godly wylle' remains absent from the sinner's acts, much as it had done in the Manichean Augustine . . . But even the most brilliant and devout theologians are capable of generating ideas whose implications have not been worked out and are in contradiction to other strands of their theology."[73]

Nonetheless, all of Julian's theology is subservient to the broader purpose of her visions. According to Julian, Christ desires that all suffering will be turned to glory and advantage by virtue of his Passion, and "to know that we do not suffer alone but with him, and to see in him our foundation, and to see that

---

70. Aers, *Salvation and Sin*, 161.
71. Aers, *Salvation and Sin*, 163–64.
72. Aers (*Salvation and Sin*, 164) does concede that "Julian is obviously, here and elsewhere, trying to counteract what she took to be punitive standards in her Church's treatment of sin and penance, ones that perhaps lacked adequate focus on God's love." Julian's willingness to depart from the established views of the church seems, in part, due to her radical experience and conviction regarding the love of God.
73. Aers, *Salvation and Sin*, 164.

his pains and his self-abnegation so far surpass all that we may suffer that it cannot be fully comprehended."[74] Julian sees the atonement as that which reflects the loving unity of the Trinity. Christ, who thirsts from "the incompleteness of his bliss" will find himself satisfied when "we who are saved" are joined to him in the eschaton.[75] Julian can speak of salvation using such intimate language, for it is the language of the Trinity itself. In the LT, Julian's reflection on the Passion has morphed into trinitarian doxology:

> And in the same revelation the Trinity suddenly filled my heart full of the utmost joy, and I understood that it will be like that in heaven forever for all those who will come there. For the Trinity is God, and God is the Trinity; and the Trinity is our maker, the Trinity is our protector, the Trinity is our everlasting lover, the Trinity is our unending joy and bliss, through our Lord Jesus Christ and in our Lord Jesus Christ.[76]

For her, the atonement is an act which heals the wounds of sin, where "all shame will be turned into honour and into greater joy."[77]

Kenotic Atonement and the Suffering God

In the modern atonement debate, there is a temptation to force a monolithic atonement paradigm onto the great theological periods of the past.[78] Remarkably, however, Julian's thinking of the atonement is more in line with modern theological thought than medieval.[79] While not rejecting the ransom and satisfaction theories of her era, she develops her atonement theology in concert

---

74. Julian, *Revelations*, 76.
75. Julian, *Revelations*, 22.
76. Julian, *Revelations*, 44.
77. Julian, *Revelations*, 25.
78. I am speaking of the various atonement theory labels used in modern theology since Gustaf Aulén's *Christus Victor*. For example, subjective vs. objective, *Christus Victor*, substitutionary, moral example, and others.
79. Tolley, "'Love was His Meaning,'" 102.

with her beliefs regarding the nature of human sin.[80] Since sin is that which allows Christ to turn shame into honor intimately, Julian's atonement theology finds no companion in that which would divorce God from creation and Christ's suffering.[81] Instead, Julian focuses her theology of the atonement regarding her belief in the absolute love and faithfulness of the triune God, a theology in keeping with her strong emphasis on Christ's unity with suffering humanity.[82] While Julian affirms that "Jesus Christ is Lord," the Lord of her vision exercises authority employing his kenosis.[83]

Julian's kenotic atonement theology is something that anticipates modern trinitarian theological insight. German theologian Eberhard Jüngel, in his book, *God as the Mystery of the World*, discusses the relationship between the Trinity and Christ's suffering as a significant correction to Christian theology:

> That the God who is love must be able to suffer and does suffer beyond all limits in the giving up of what is most authentically his for the sake of mortal man, is an indispensable insight of the newer theology schooled by Luther's Christology and Hegel's philosophy. Only the God who is identical with the Crucified one makes us certain of his love and thus of himself.[84]

For Jüngel, the implications of the crucified God are an insight of modern theology and fundamental to one's conception of God:

> When we attempt to think of God as the one who communicates and expresses himself in the person Jesus, then we must always remember that this man was crucified, that he was killed in the name of God's law. For responsible usage of the word 'God,' the Crucified One is virtually the real definition of what is meant with the word 'God.'[85]

---

80. Tolley, "'Love was His Meaning,'" 106.
81. Tolley, "'Love was His Meaning,'" 106.
82. Tolley, "'Love was His Meaning,'" 106.
83. Heath, "Judgement Without Wrath," 45.
84. Jüngel, *God as the Mystery*, 373.
85. Jüngel, *God as the Mystery*, 13.

For the medieval Julian, such a concept was hardly novel. Likewise, German theologian Jürgen Moltmann, in his book *The Crucified God* articulates his theology of hope in terms of Christ's suffering. Moltmann, whom himself lived in the era of "the hells of world wars, the hells of Auschwitz, Hiroshima and Vietnam," places the crucified God as the central component of Christian theology.[86] Moltmann's experiences led him to consider the nature of God's response to a sinful and suffering world. God, according to Moltmann, is one who responds to suffering by becoming suffering:

> God's being is in suffering and the suffering is in God's being itself, because God is love. It takes the 'metaphysical rebellion' up into itself because it recognizes in the cross of Christ a rebellion in metaphysics, or better, a rebellion in God himself: God himself loves and suffers the death of Christ in his love. He is no 'cold heavenly power,' nor does he 'tread his way over corpses,' but is known as the human God in the crucified Son of Man.[87]

Before applying modern concepts of God to medieval ones, one must recognize the danger of harmonizing theological thought across historical contexts. To begin, Julian's reflection on the suffering triune God is hardly an academic endeavour but a devotional one. Furthermore, the questions Julian concerns herself with are the result of a deeply personal vision and not out of intellectual curiosity. There remains a sizeable methodological chasm between one who ponders God in an anchoritic cell and one who performs theology in an ivory tower. Nonetheless, all three of these individuals share a common concern for communicating the nature and economy of God in terms of emphasizing God's identification with human suffering.

In chapter 20 of *Revelations*, Julian communicates what she believes to be the three things worth remembering about Christ's Passion: "For the most fundamental implication to consider in the Passion is to recognize and comprehend what he is who suffered, also bearing in mind two lesser considerations: one is what

---

86. Moltmann, *The Crucified God*, 319.
87. Moltmann, *The Crucified God*, 332–33.

he suffered, and the other is for whom he suffered."[88] Considering what he is who suffered, Julian remarks that "he who is highest and noblest was brought most low and most utterly despised."[89] Regarding what he suffered and for whom he suffered, Julian explains that:

> For just as he was most tender and pure, so he was strongest and most mighty to suffer. And he suffered for the sins of everyone who shall be saved; and he saw everyone's sorrow and desolation and sorrowed out of kindness and love . . . For as long as he was liable to suffer, he suffered for us and sorrowed for us; and now he is risen again and no longer liable to suffering, he still suffers with us.[90]

According to Julian, God resurrected Christ as one who "still suffers with us." According to Moltmann, Christ constitutes his loving existence through the God-forsaken event of the cross, a type of suffering "which justifies the godless, fills the forsaken with love and even brings the dead alive."[91] For both Julian and Moltmann, God's Trinitarian love "for us" is demonstrated through God's suffering on the cross.

Central to this trinitarian understanding for Julian is the revelation of the motherliness of God.[92] In describing the Second Person of the Trinity, Julian writes:

> The Second Person of the Trinity is our mother in nature, in our substantial creation, in whom we are grounded and rooted, and he is our mother in mercy by taking on our sensory being. And so our mother—in whom the parts of us are kept undivided—works within us in various ways; for in our mother, Christ, we profit and grow, and in mercy he reforms and restores us, and, by virtue of his Passion and his death and resurrection, he unites us to our substance. So our mother acts mercifully to all his children who are submissive and obedient to him.[93]

88. Julian, *Revelations*, 67.
89. Julian, *Revelations*, 67.
90. Julian, *Revelations*, 67.
91. Moltmann, *The Crucified God*, 361.
92. Dearborn, "The Crucified Christ," 289.
93. Julian, *Revelations*, 127.

Elsewhere, Julian elaborates on how unity with Christ our "mother" effects humanity:

> And in his taking on of our nature he gave us life; in his blessed dying upon the cross he gave birth to us into eternal life; and from that time, and now, and forever until the day of judgement, he feeds us and fosters us, just as the great and supreme lovingness of motherhood and the natural need of childhood require. Lovely and precious is our heavenly mother in the sight of our soul; precious and lovely are the children of grace in the sight of our heavenly mother, with gentleness and meekness, and all the lovely virtues which belong to children by nature; for naturally the child does not despair of the mother's love; naturally the child does not presume to act by itself; naturally the child loves its mother, and each loves the other; these, and all others that are like them, are the fair virtues with which our heavenly mother is honoured and pleased.[94]

When these two realities are considered together, Julian's inability to perceive of God's wrath and judgment and her hope that all shall be well and all manner of things shall be well, the image of motherhood opens up as a meaningful metaphor to explain her revelation.[95] The relationship between Christ the "mother" and

---

94. Julian, *Revelations*, 135–36.

95. Julian explicitly addresses God's lack of anger on three occasions in *Revelations*: "But there can be no anger in God, as it seems to me, for our good Lord has regard eternally for his own glory and the benefit of all who shall be saved. With power and justice he withstands the reprobates who, out of malice and malignity, busy themselves to scheme and to act against God's will" (*Revelations*, 58). Later, Julian (*Revelations*, 102) states: "For I saw no anger except on man's part, and he forgives that in us; for anger is nothing else but a resistance and contrariness to peace and to love, and it comes either from lack of strength, or from lack of wisdom, or from lack of goodness—and this lack is not in God, but it is on our part; for through sin and wretchedness we have in us a wretched and continual resistance to peace and to love, and he revealed this very often in his loving expression of pity and compassion; for the foundation of mercy is love, and the operation of mercy is to safeguard us in love; and this was revealed in such a way that I could not discern any aspect of mercy other than in love alone—that is to say, as it appeared to me." Finally, Julian (*Revelations*, 104) concludes, "And so when we, through the working of mercy and grace, are made humble and gentle, we are completely safe. Suddenly the soul is united to God when it is truly at peace in itself, for no anger is to be found in God."

his children is one of "natural love" where the child does not despair the mother's love. In the tumultuous world in which Julian lived, one need see God as Father, but also God as Mother, a Mother who protects, nourishes, and loves his children regardless of what wretched state they may find themselves in.[96] Considering Julian's strong emphasis on Christ's unity with humanity, the intimate language of Mother emerges as that which captures her understanding of Christ.

The concept of God as Mother was not a new idea in Julian's era. Anselm, in a famous song still used in The Church of England's common book of prayer, writes:

> Jesus, like a mother you gather your people to you;
> you are gentle with us as a mother with her children.
> Often you weep over our sins and our pride,
> tenderly you draw us from hatred and judgement.
> You comfort us in sorrow and bind up our wounds,
> in sickness you nurse us, and with pure milk you feed us.
> Jesus, by your dying we are born to new life;
> by your anguish and labour we come forth in joy.
> Despair turns to hope through your sweet goodness;
> through your gentleness we find comfort in fear.
> Your warmth gives life to the dead,
> your touch makes sinners righteous.
> Lord Jesus, in your mercy heal us;
> in your love and tenderness remake us.
> In your compassion bring grace and forgiveness,
> for the beauty of heaven may your love prepare us.[97]

Julian, like Anselm, applies God's Motherhood to the atoning sacrifice of Christ. What better way to express the new birth through Christ's death than with the imagery of labour pains?[98] What image of eucharistic "nourishment" in Julian's Catholic medieval world can trump the image of a mother feeding her

---

96. Throughout Julian's usage of Mother as a descriptor in *Revelations*, she always maintains the masculine pronoun for Christ in keeping with Orthodox tradition.
97. Anselm, "A Song of Anselm," [n.d.].
98. Dearborn, "The Crucified Christ," 293.

child?[99] However, unlike Anselm, Julian allows this metaphor to inform one's self-perception as a sinner:

> The mother may allow the child to fall sometimes and be hurt in various ways for its own benefit, but because of her love she can never allow any kind of danger to befall the child. And even though our earthly mother may let her child perish, our heavenly mother Jesus may not allow us who are his children to perish; for he is almighty, all wisdom, and all love, and so is none but he—blessed may he be![100]

For Julian, our falling is not disastrous, and God is not angry, for just as a mother allows her children to fall, so too does God our Mother to allow humanity to walk and eventually run back to God.[101]

Applying Julian Today

Through modern eyes, Julian of Norwich is an enigma—libraries dedicate stacks of biographies to the important individuals of our time, but here is a woman whose real name we do not know expounding intimate mysteries of the Trinity. What is one to make of a mystical revelation of an anchorite from the fourteenth century?

Jürgen Moltmann tells the story of when he was a prisoner of war during World War II at the young age of twenty. After reading the cry of dereliction of the suffering Christ on the cross, he describes an experience where he was "found by God," as if God himself was speaking "to him with bloodied and parched lips in cries of pain and abandonment, bitter fruits of seemingly misplaced trust."[102] Sometimes when the world is wrong, the only answer for suffering is to look towards the suffering Christ. In Julian's broken world and from her small cell, she pondered what it meant to be a child of God: "So in our Father, God almighty, we have our being; and in our mother through mercy we

---

99. Dearborn, "The Crucified Christ," 293.
100. Julian, *Revelations*, 132.
101. Soskice, *The Kindness of God*, 144.
102. Moltmann, *The Crucified God*, ix.

have our reforming and restoring, in whom our parts are united and all made perfect man; and by the rewards and gracious gift of the Holy Spirit we are made complete."[103] In our broken world, what is the suffering Christ speaking to us about being a child of God?

Julian's theology begins and ends with God's love. Just as Julian pondered the meaning of her revelation, recognizing that this love was not for her alone but all of God's children, we too must look outward as the Spirit works inward. Julian was convinced that to be whole one must encounter the love of the triune God and experience God as both Father and Mother in unity through the Holy Spirit. An advantage for Julian was a deeply ingrained religious context to develop her theology, but one in which she was prepared to challenge when it did not fit her experience. Experience, while not entirely reliable as a foundation for theology, has the potential to begin a journey towards meaningful questions and answers. For Julian, her question was the meaning of sin in the context of God's love. For us today, however, an experience is not often the starting point of a journey, but an end in of itself. As we preach Christ, and Christ crucified in the context not of a religious culture, but a culture of consumerism, that large image of God's love is reduced to individual applicability. While Julian's theology lacks the sophistication of a modern systematic theologian, it returns one to the heart of Christian theology: "its capacity to point to the living triune God and articulate the kind of life we should live in response to his revelation."[104]

Conclusion

Julian reminds us to communicate Christ's atonement as carefully and as meaningful as possible. In a world where a caricature of the cross is morally repugnant to many, Julian offers an image not of a wrathful Father God punishing Christ on the cross for sin, but of something far more solicitous. For Julian, "the blessed

---

103. Julian, *Revelations*, 128.
104. Kapic, "Has Academic Theology Lost its Way?" [n.p.].

wounds of our Saviour are open and rejoice to heal us; the sweet, gracious hands of our mother are ready and enfold us diligently; for in all this he performs the role of a kindly nurse who has nothing else to do but attend to the safety of her child."[105]

Atonement debates will continue to rage on. Theories will form, reform, be abandoned or corrected. Nonetheless, the love of Christ must remain in all. Thankfully, in Julian we get a glimpse of hope, one in which Christ's love blinds sin and every child of God is safe from the spectre of Black Deaths, fragmented churches, World Wars, and suffering of every kind.

Bibliography

Aers, David. *Salvation and Sin*. Notre Dame: University of Notre Dame Press, 2009.

Anselm. "A Song of Anselm," *The Church of England*, [n.d.], https://www.churchofengland.org/prayer-and-worship/worship-texts-and-resources/common-worship/daily-prayer/canticles-daily-prayer/82-song-anselm.

———. "Why God Became Man." In *Anselm of Canterbury: The Major Works*, edited by Brian Davies and G. R. Evans, 260–355. Reissue edition. Oxford: Oxford University Press, 1998.

Augustine. *City of God*, edited by Paul A. Böer. Kindle Edition. New York: Veritatis Splendor, 2012.

Aulén, Gustaf. *Christus Victor: An Historical Study of the Three Main Types of the Idea of the Atonement*. Eugene, OR: Wipf & Stock, 2003.

---

105. Julian, *Revelations*, 133.

Bennett, Thomas Andrew. "Julian of Norwich, the Bible, and Creative, Orthodox Theology: Always Novel, Never New." *Scottish Journal of Theology* 69 (2016) 309–25.

Cooper, Austin. *Julian Of Norwich*. London: Burns & Oats, 2001.

Dearborn, Kerry. "The Crucified Christ as the Motherly God: The Theology of Julian of Norwich." *Scottish Journal of Theology* 55 (2002) 283–302.

The Editors of Encyclopaedia Britannica. "Julian of Norwich." In *Encyclopædia Britannica*. Online: https://www.britannica.com/biography/Julian-of-Norwich.

Frykholm, Amy. *Julian of Norwich: A Contemplative Biography*. Brewster, MA: Paraclete, 2013.

Healy-Varley, Margaret. "Wounds Shall Be Worships: Anselm in Julian of Norwich's Revelation of Love." *The Journal of English and Germanic Philology* 115 (2016) 186–212.

Heath, Elaine A. "Judgment Without Wrath: Christus Victor in 'The Servant Parable.'" *Ashland Theological Journal* (1998) 37–50.

Jantzen, Grace. *Julian of Norwich*. London: SPCK, 1987.

Julian. *Revelations of Divine Love*. Translated by Barry Windeatt. Kindle edition. Oxford: Oxford University Press, 2015.

Jüngel, Eberhard. *God as the Mystery of the World: On the Foundation of the Theology of the Crucified One in the Dispute Between Theism and Atheism*. London: Bloomsbury, 2014.

Kapic, Kelly M. "Has Academic Theology Lost Its Way?" *Christianity Today*, March 22, 2019, Online: https://www.

christianitytoday.com/ct/2019/march-web-only/mirolsav-volf-matthew-croasmun-life-world-theology.html.

Law, Sarah. "In the Centre: Spiritual and Cultural Representations of Julian Norwich in the Julian Centre." In *Julian of Norwich's Legacy: Medieval Mysticism and Post-Medieval Reception*, edited by Sarah Salih and Denise N. Baker, 173–90. The New Middle Ages. New York: Palgrave Macmillan, 2009.

Moltmann, Jurgen. *The Crucified God: 40th Anniversary Edition*. Minneapolis: Fortress, 2015.

Nuth, Joan M. "Two Medieval Soteriologies: Anselm of Canterbury and Julian of Norwich." *Theological Studies* 53 (1992) 611–45.

———. *Wisdom's Daughter*. New York: Crossroad, 1991.

Rolf, Veronica Mary. *An Explorer's Guide to Julian of Norwich*. Downers Grove, IL: InterVarsity, 2018.

Shea, Mary Lou. *Medieval Women on Sin and Salvation: Hadewijch of Antwerp, Beatrice of Nazareth, Margaret Ebner, and Julian of Norwich*. American University Studies. New York: Peter Lang, 2010.

Soskice, Janet Martin. *The Kindness of God: Metaphor, Gender, and Religious Language*. Oxford: Oxford University Press, 2007.

Tolley, George. "'Love Was His Meaning' Julian of Norwich and Atonement." *Theology* 111 (2008) 102–7.

Turner, Denys. *Julian of Norwich, Theologian*. New Haven, CT: Yale University Press, 2011.

Walters, Gwenfair M. "The Atonement in Medieval Theology." In *The Glory of the Atonement: Biblical, Theological and Practical Perspectives*, edited by Charles E. Hill and Frank A. James III, 239–62. Downers Grove, IL: InterVarsity, 2004.

Watson, Nicholas, and Jacqueline Jenkins, eds. *The Writings of Julian of Norwich: A Vision Showed to a Devout Woman and a Revelation of Love*. University Park, PA: Pennsylvania State University Press, 2006.

Maundy Thursday, All the World is Still

Malcolm Guite[1]
University of Cambridge, Cambridge, UK

Maundy Thursday, all the world is still
The planes wait, grounded by departure gates
The street is empty and the shopping mall
Deserted. Padlocked, the playground waits
Against the day that children play again
Till then our sad refrain is just refrain.

Maundy Thursday, all the world is still
And Jesus is at supper with his friends
No longer in the upper room, that hall
In Zion where the story starts and ends,
For he descended from it long ago
To find his new friends in the here and now.

Maundy Thursday, all the world is still
And Jesus is at supper with his friends
Our doors are locked for fear, but he has skill
In breaking barriers. With ease he bends
Our prison bars, slips past the sentry post
And joins us as the guest who is our host.

Maundy Thursday, all the world is still
But in cramped quarters on the fifteenth floor,

---

1. Malcolm Guite is a life-fellow of Girton College in the University of Cambridge. He is the author of *Faith, Hope, & Poetry* (Routledge, 2008) and *Mariner: A Voyage with Samuel Taylor Coleridge* (Hodder & Stoughton, 2017). His newest poetry collection is *After Prayer: New Sonnets and Other Poems* (Canterbury, 2019).

In lonely towers made of glass and steel,
And in the fierce favelas of the poor,
Touching with wounded hands the wounds he tends
Christ Jesus is at supper with his friends.

BLESSED ARE THE PEACEMAKERS: CANADIAN PENTECOSTALISM
AND MILITARY CONFLICT IN THE EARLY TWENTIETH CENTURY

Geoffrey Butler
Wycliffe College, University of Toronto, Toronto, ON, Canada

One of the age-old debates within the Christian church concerns the believer's role in national conflict. While certain traditions have historically viewed military participation as permissible or even praiseworthy, others have denounced it as antithetical to the teachings of Christ and a capitulation to the kingdoms of this world. With the commencement of World War I, the Pentecostal movement, still in its infancy, was forced to grapple intensely with this issue.[1] Within the North American context, this was especially true in Canada, who entered the conflict three years earlier than its neighbor to the south. Little more than twenty years later, Pentecostals would be required to consider the question again during the Second World War. While not typically a topic of discussion among Canadian Pentecostals today, it bears asking: Where has the tradition historically stood on this issue? How ought a Christian to respond when military service is requested or even required? Perhaps looking into the past may give contemporary Pentecostals a pattern to follow in the present. This paper will explore the pacifist sentiment that permeated early Pentecostalism, with special attention granted to the conversation within Canada concerning the response to the challenges brought on by two world wars in the first half of the twentieth century. It

---

1. While the focus of this paper will be on the attitude of Canadian Pentecostals toward the first two World Wars, given the deep historical ties that they share with American Pentecostals—as well as the relatively small size of the movement at that time period when compared to the twenty-first century—voices from both sides of the border will be considered as part of this survey, especially in exploring the earliest roots of the movement.

will also highlight the shift that took place during the interwar years and explore the how Pentecostalism, for the most part, came to abandon its pacifist roots by the late 1940s. It will argue that its downfall was largely due to other larger concerns of the movement—namely, evangelism and missions—along with the gradual mainstreaming of Pentecostalism within Christendom. As evidenced by this shift in attitude, it seems clear that through the influence of other Christian traditions, Pentecostalism came to resemble mainstream evangelicalism on this point more closely in the middle of the century than it had in the beginning.

The Roots of Nonviolence

The established presence of Wesleyan, Holiness, Mennonite, and Anabaptist thought in the movement all help explain why pacifist attitudes so strongly permeated Pentecostalism.[2] In a 1994 monograph, Thomas William Miller notes that the first generation of the Pentecostal Assemblies of Canada (PAOC) contained many converts from such backgrounds, all of which registered as conscientious objectors during national conflict.[3] Like their predecessors, first-generation Pentecostals viewed allegiance to the state, not as a virtue, but a threat to the believer's commitment to the kingdom of God;[4] viewing their ultimate citizenship as heavenly, some went so far as to label patriotism as a grave sin.[5] Numerous observers have identified the importance of understanding early Pentecostal ecclesiology for comprehending this perspective. John Howard Yoder, for example, points out that, like the nineteenth-century restorationist movements, they were

---

2. See Dayton, *An Historical Survey*, 6–7. For many Holiness believers, who strongly emphasized entire sanctification and "radical holiness" as adapted from earlier Methodist thought, going to war on behalf of an earthly kingdom appeared inconsistent with the goal of separation from the world.

3. Miller, *Canadian Pentecostals*, 45–46. Numerous early Canadian Pentecostal leaders were formerly affiliated with the Mennonite Brethren Church, a denomination eventually granted conscientious objector status during World War I.

4. Wacker, *Heaven Below*, 242–44.

5. Shuman, "Pentecost and the End," 74–75.

fiercely opposed to anything that could be perceived as "worldliness" and exhibited what he labels a "literal obedience to Scripture without rationalizing."[6] To put it another way, they simply took the Bible at face value, committing to practice what they believed it taught regardless of the prevailing culture's opinion of them. It was a commonly held opinion among the Pentecostals that part of the reason for the church's moral decline in the fourth and fifth centuries laid in its political involvement with the Roman Empire. By entangling itself with the affairs of the state, including its military, it had unwittingly given rise to a structure of Christendom that betrayed basic principles of the faith. As Joel Shuman has observed:

> Pentecostals of the early twentieth century saw themselves as being the contemporary restoration of the New Testament church, a community that had become increasingly unfaithful in the time between the Pentecost of the first century and that of the twentieth. Central to the church's fall during that interim era was its entry into political establishmentarianism . . . This disestablishment was accentuated by the initial rejection of Pentecostals by the evangelical mainstream. This rejection served to enforce their tendency to see themselves as being citizens not of any earthly nation, but of the kingdom of God.[7]

Their conviction that believers ought to be distinct from society may have stemmed partially from the fact they were outsiders even within Christendom.[8] Of particular interest is Shuman's comment about evangelicalism's rejection of the Pentecostal movement.[9] Initially frowned upon by the mainstream, the early Pentecostals felt little discomfort viewing themselves as

---

6. Yoder, *Christian Attitudes*, 261.
7. Shuman, "Pentecost and the End," 75–76.
8. Hauerwas, "Foreword," xiii notes as much by observing that "the early Pentecostal movements represented a restorationist ecclesiology that inclined the church toward a pacifist orientation. The nonviolence of the early Pentecostal movement was first and foremost understood to be an ecclesial commitment."
9. See Althouse, "Canadian Pentecostal Pacifism," 41. The author goes on to cite the increasing favor Pentecostals enjoyed both with established denominations and the governing authorities as a catalyst for the shift away from a position of nonresistance.

outsiders.[10] It is undeniable that in its infancy the movement contained a strong anti-establishment flavor; in light of Pentecostal positions on tongues, healing, racial unity, and other issues that were quite countercultural for the day; perhaps, the opposition to military participation ought not to be too shocking. They saw themselves returning to the biblical standard that the historic church had, for the most part, ignored or forgotten, along with several other distinctives. The consensus was that Scripture forbade violence against other individuals, and due to a literal hermeneutic that characterized the movement, they took such passages at face value.[11] It may be summarized that most Pentecostals perceived two major barriers to military service. The first was that it required devoting one's allegiance to an earthly kingdom. Viewing themselves as citizens of a heavenly kingdom, they instinctively recoiled at such a notion.[12] Secondly, military service was perceived as incompatible with the call of Christ to a nonviolent way of life. Yet, like other peace movements before them, the Pentecostals would soon be forced to put their theology into practice with the emergence of a conflict the likes of which the world had never seen.

World War I: Response to Conflict

World War I represented the first major, practical challenge to the young Pentecostal movement's commitment to pacifism. The question of military service was no longer a theoretical matter but an inescapable problem. While a distinct subset of Pentecostalism in its own right, the Canadian branch was heavily influenced by other Canadian denominations as well as by American Pentecostalism. The outbreak illustrated that the influence of the latter extended not only to core distinctives like Spirit baptism and divine healing but also to military involvement. In 1914—the year the war began and the denomination was founded—the Assemblies of God included an unequivocally pacifist resolution

---

10. Shuman, "Pentecost and the End," 75–76.
11. Shuman, "Pentecost and the End," 73.
12. Shuman, "Pentecost and the End," 75.

in its constitution, stating that believers could not uphold the teaching of Christ to love one's enemy while taking human life.[13] Canadian Pentecostals released no such official statement, as the PAOC did not exist at the time. Yet, they were strongly impacted by Americans such as Frank Bartleman, who, as he traveled across the nation as an itinerant preacher,[14] denounced the conflict so strongly that he evoked suspicion from some that he was a German sympathizer.[15] There may be several reasons why he in particular expressed such strong opposition. Just prior to the beginning of the conflict in 1914, he had traveled throughout Europe to meet fellow Pentecostals involved in missions work in the UK, Germany, Russia, and other countries.[16] Having seen God move in a nation such as Germany, now an enemy in the eyes of his own government, it is understandable why Bartleman would have viewed the conflict as a hindrance to the mission of the church. Moreover, as for his political convictions, he was convinced that capitalism was in and of itself a corrupt system;[17] therefore, those nations—and churches—that fought to defend it were also corrupt.[18] However, it seems clear that his concerns were first and foremost theological. Not only was his mother a Quaker, but before joining the Pentecostal movement Bartleman frequently ministered among Holiness, Wesleyans, and Anabaptists, all of which would have

13. "Combined Minutes [1914]," 10–11. The subsequent 1916 minutes, however, also condemn animosity toward the federal government and stipulated that those who dishonored the flag would have their credentials revoked (*Combined Minutes* [1916], 23). Therefore, the unwillingness to take up arms is clearly not intended as an act of disloyalty but rather an exercise of religious liberty.
14. Althouse, "Canadian Pentecostal Pacifism," 34–35.
15. Beaman, *Pentecostal Pacifism*, 58. The author notes that one of Bartleman's tracts appeared so pro-German that "the editor of the *Christian Evangel* called upon readers to destroy (it)."
16. Beaman, *Pentecostal Pacifism*, 56.
17. Althouse, "Canadian Pentecostal Pacifism," 32–33.
18. See Bartleman, "War and the Christian," 5. In an article published shortly after the outset of the war, he blasts war as a hindrance to foreign missions and flatly declares that "a 'war church' is a harlot church."

contained a strong bent toward nonviolence.[19] Bartleman, perhaps most notable for his bold statements, was in no way unique in his sentiment.[20] Many early Pentecostal leaders were convinced that a rejection of nationalism would be crucial if Pentecostalism was to remain a truly international movement. Crossing borders with the good news, they reasonably deduced, would be much more feasible without the hindrance of armed conflict or even suspicion of foreign nationals.

The question remains of how such attitudes in the broader movement uniquely affected Canadian Pentecostals. As previously noted, they were in the company of other pacifist groups in Canadas such as Quakers, Mennonites, and some Methodists, all proclaiming themselves conscientious objectors. Some, such as the Quakers, went so far as to refuse paying taxes that would fund the war effort.[21] Still in its infancy, Pentecostals were denied conscientious objector status and therefore were not legally exempted from service. George Chambers, the first General Superintendent of the PAOC, notes that numerous young Pentecostal men who declined to serve, and thus were found to violate the 1917 *Military Service Act*,[22] were imprisoned in Kingston, Ontario; a punishment that, due to horrific mistreatment, resulted in the death of at least one man.[23] Murray Dempster, in a 2013 piece on Canadian Pentecostal pacifism in the two World Wars, documents further accounts of persecution and torture of conscientious objectors, including one particularly heinous incident involving a Pentecostal which took place at the Minto Street Barracks in Winnipeg. During this particular incident:

> Three conscientious objectors—Charles Matheson, a Pentecostal, and Robert Clegg and Frank Naish, both members of the International Bible Students Association (IBSA)—were sentenced to three days

---

19. Robeck Jr., "Bartleman, Frank," 366.
20. See Dempster, "Crossing Borders," 121–42, cited in Alexander, ed., *Pentecostals and Nonviolence*, 123–25. The author lists no less than five major early leaders in the Pentecostal movement who were absolute pacifists
21. Socknat, "Conscientious Objectors," 61–63.
22. Canada Department of Justice, "Military Service Act."
23. Chambers, *50 Years*, 55–56.

> confinement for their unwillingness to obey a lawful command . . . All three, in turn, were forcibly stripped naked and held under ice-cold showers until they either surrendered to military authority or collapsed. Pentecostal Matheson was first. After standing firm for hours in refusing to comply, he finally buckled under the unrelenting pressure and agreed to submit to military orders. Clegg and Naish followed. Their severe punishment ended with Naish in a state of nervous collapse and Clegg in an unconscious state, being admitted to the hospital.[24]

Even more severely, David Wells, another young Pentecostal Bible student in Winnipeg during the war, was arrested on account of his refusal to serve and imprisoned at Stony Mountain Penitentiary. Just days after his arrival, he was admitted to the Selkirk Asylum on account of his poor mental condition and died shortly thereafter, with many suspecting that brutal treatment at the prison may well have contributed to his breakdown and eventual death.[25] While some others avoided such a fate by participating in non-combat roles,[26] it seems that Canadian Pentecostals ultimately paid dearly for the fact they had not registered in any official capacity with the Canadian government. Since the American Assemblies of God had done so, they enjoyed, at least in theory, a measure of legal protection not afforded to their Canadian counterparts.

Despite such strong rhetoric denouncing the conflict, it must also be noted that Canadian Pentecostals were not as resolutely pacifist as their American neighbors. As briefly mentioned prior, Canada, in contrast to the US, remained a commonwealth nation with strong ties to the British Crown and, by extension, the Church of England, which strongly supported the war.[27] This was true not only of denominational leaders or clergy; Melissa Davidson, in a 2014 essay, highlights the immense contribution made by its laypersons by noting that:

---

24. Dempster, "The Canada—Britain—USA," 7–8.
25. Penton, "Wells, David."
26. Miller, *Canadian Pentecostals*, 46.
27. See Althouse, "Canadian Pentecostal Pacifism," 36–37.

In the fall of 1916, when the Canadian government released a report detailing the religious affiliations of recruits in the CEF, Anglicans made up roughly 40 percent of the CEF with 165,145 men in uniform. With a total declared population of just over one million—about 15 percent of the overall Canadian population—Canadian Anglicans were clearly enlisting in numbers disproportionate to their overall population.[28]

Within the official state Church of England, the war effort was perceived as necessary to protect Christian values and defend a truly righteous cause—British imperialism.[29] "Canadian Anglicans," she notes, "were bound up with other Anglicans in Britain and throughout the Empire."[30] However, this patriotic fervor was hardly limited to the Anglican fold; in the late nineteenth century, Presbyterian churchman G. M. Grant, a strong proponent of the missionary endeavor and the role of religion in public life, called for a form of Christian unity in Canada that defined the role of the church as inextricably linked to that of the state. As Berger explains:

> Imperial unity and church unity were, in Grant's mind, not merely analogous processes—they were both products of identical causes and directed to the same end. Just as the union of the church was the precondition for the Christianization of the social order, so too the unity of the Empire was necessary to maintain a political power making for righteousness on earth. Both Christianity and imperialism called men to self-sacrifice and service; both required the allegiance to ideals and the denigration of the material and the flesh.[31]

It is on account of this conviction that Grant, as well as many of his contemporaries, supported the British Empire's Boer War in South Africa less than two decades before the First World War.[32] At the turn of the century, images of the British flag,

---

28. Davidson, "The Anglican Church," 153.
29. Davidson, "The Anglican Church," 155–56.
30. Davidson, "The Anglican Church," 167.
31. Berger, *Sense of Power*, 34.
32. Although, as Berger (*Sense of Power*, 35) notes, Grant himself was "one of the last Canadian imperialists to support the British government against

songs about the glories of the Empire, and a sense of identity tied to the imperial project meant that any threat to Britain was a threat to Canada too.[33] Carman Miller notes that, "In the case of the war in South Africa, the churches were firmly convinced of the superiority of the British race, and its institutions," and goes on to highlight that few Canadian Christians were willing to question the war precisely because of their steadfast loyalty to such ideals. "Since Canadian identity was so closely identified with Britain and the empire," he explains, "to admit that the war was not just was to raise serious questions about the very essence of Canadian identity."[34] This illustrates the sense of connection Canadians felt to their mother country as a young nation. Even by 1914, when Britain entered the war, it had been less than 50 years since confederation; should it come as a surprise, then, that neither Canada nor most of its churches would perceive any daylight between its own interests and those of the Crown? Even the Baptists, a free church tradition with a history of stressing the separation between church and state, voiced support for Britain shortly after the outbreak of the war—a stance which grew stronger in the face of reported German atrocities as the conflict carried on.[35]

Thus, a strong sense of loyalty to the Empire was already ubiquitous in Canadian society prior to entering the First World War, an action that only further intensified loyalty. North of the border sat a nation under fifty years old that identified as part of a worldwide commonwealth united under Britain. South of the border was a much more established country that not only rebelled against the British to gain independence well over a century prior but that still largely favored an isolationist foreign policy.[36] Indeed, the United States did not even enter the war until 1917—three years after their neighbors had done so, and even then, with divided public opinion. Thus, not only can a stronger

the Boers," and only changed his position upon determining that "the survival of the Empire was at stake."
33. Crouse, "Canada's Salvation Army," 89–90.
34. Miller, "Writing Religious Minorities," 27–28.
35. See Haykin and Clary, "O God of Battles," 173–74.
36. See Heath, "American Churches," 2.

bent toward pacifism be explained by the lack of any American connection to the Crown, but also by the fact that they were not at war at all until relatively close to its end. Despite their pacifist roots and instincts, the loyalty to the British Empire that most Canadians felt was a significant factor that American Pentecostals would have no reason to consider. The robust imperialist sentiment that permeated more established denominations and, indeed, Canadian society at large was bound to exert significant influence on Canadian Pentecostalism. In the United States, on the other hand, the government had to be wary of religious opposition; not only was there no state church to support its efforts, as with the Church of England, but American authorities had also been subject to criticism from some Christian groups during previous military campaigns that they did not feel were justified.[37] Early twentieth-century America, then, proved a more hospitable environment for Pentecostal pacifism than Canada. It is little wonder that there are no records of Canadian Pentecostals such as R. E. McAlister or George Chambers—despite the Holiness roots of the former and the Quaker background of the latter—openly making statements expressing sympathy with the German cause or painting them as the least culpable in the conflict as in the case of the American Frank Bartleman.[38] Doing so would have invited charges of disloyalty toward the Crown which, despite their unwillingness to take up arms, Canadian Pentecostals wished to avoid. While their American counterparts could make bold statements denouncing military participation for the better part of the conflict, knowing their own countrymen had no part in it, Canadians enjoyed no such luxury.[39] Obviously, making bold statements about the immorality of military involvement is much easier when your nation is not at war. At a time when the

37. Heath, "American Churches," 3.
38. Beaman, *Pentecostal Pacifism*, 58.
39. The Americans did not formally declare war on Germany until 6 April 1917, a mere year and a half before the war ended. Though the British, like other Europeans, "were stunned by the sudden onset of war in the summer of 1914, Americans experienced an altogether different situation," with the nation declaring "neutrality at the outbreak of war." See Heath, "American Churches," 1.

Americans were still neutral in the conflict, Canadian Pentecostals had already been denied conscientious objector status and had been subjected to imprisonment and other forms of persecution. Therefore, while the Assemblies of God eventually did affirm the divine ordination of government and their personal loyalty to the US upon its entry to the war,[40] Canadian Pentecostals experienced a much deeper sense of tension between their faith and their civic obligation—and thus, even had they been as formally organized as their American counterparts, in all likelihood their opposition still would have been rather tepid in comparison.

The Interwar Period

Between the World Wars, pacifist sentiment remained widespread in the Pentecostal movement on both sides of the border. When the PAOC received government charter in May 1919, one of its stated purposes was "To exercise any of the powers usually conferred on duly incorporated benevolent societies by either Dominion or Provincial authority."[41] Though no explicit reference is made to war, peace, or conscientious objection, given that the letter's patent was drafted only six months after the war's end it seems reasonable to deduce the framers of the document viewed legal protection and religious liberty as key benefits of obtaining a charter. In 1920, with the establishment of a denominational publication, *The Pentecostal Testimony*, PAOC adherents had a platform from which to promote their doctrinal distinctives for the first time in their history. The first edition, printed in December of that year, explained that, "The publishing of a Canadian Pentecostal paper has been a keen felt need for a long time, as there is not a Canadian paper in the Dominion."[42] With the formal establishment of the denomination, Canadian Pentecostals were also enabled to construct doctrinal statements and resolutions like the Americans, which extended to matters of war and peace. At their 1928 General Conference, the fellowship

---

40. Shuman, "Pentecost and the End," 76.
41. "Minutes of the Pentecostal Assemblies."
42. "The Paper," *Canadian Pentecostal Testimony*, December 1920, 4.

declared itself to be a pacifist organization in their *Statement of Fundamental Truths*, thus marking the first time the PAOC released such a statement. The fellowship declared participation in war to be against "New Testament teaching and principles as prohibiting Christians from shedding blood or taking human life," and asserted that Pentecostals would not "take up any weapon or destruction to slay another, whether in our own defense, or in defense of others."[43] Accordingly, the PAOC, at about the halfway point between the two world wars, remained so averse to violence as to even rule out self-defense in its exposition of "fundamental truths."

The end of the First World War also ushered in a time when opposition to war became widespread among Canadian Christendom at large, undoubtedly due at least in part to dismay over the global catastrophe it had just witnessed.[44] This contributed to clergy outside of peace church movements calling for abstention from armed conflict, contributing to a somewhat more hospitable environment for groups such as the Pentecostals.[45] Within their own circles, the transition into a time of peace did not put an end to the denunciation of military involvement by itinerant preachers. Frank Bartleman published a brief 1922 tract in which he blasted ecclesial bodies which held to just war theory as "apostate";[46] however, having already, at other points, referred to such churches as "harlots" and associated them with the spirit of the Antichrist,[47] perhaps this charge could be considered rather tame in comparison. Yet, it also shows that the Pentecostal opposition to violence was not just an opportunistic tool used during actual periods of conflict; this was an issue the movement saw as part of their separation from the world. Nor was such interwar sentiment limited to Americans such as Bartleman; Donald Gee, a British conscientious objector during the War who frequently penned articles in North American Pentecostal periodicals, wrote

43. "Statement of Fundamental Truths," 5.
44. Heath, "Canadian Churches and War," 80.
45. McCutcheon et al., *The Christian and War*.
46. Bartleman, "Christian Citizenship."
47. Bartleman, "War and the Christian," 4.

a 1930 article for *The Pentecostal Evangel* entitled "War, the Bible, and the Christian." In the aftermath of the First World War, the now-defunct League of Nations had been founded in the hope of securing lasting world peace. While Gee conceded that the support of this endeavor by "the nominal churches of Christendom" was "the only possible attitude consistent with the spirit and teaching of Jesus Christ," he was also quick to point out the utter failure of such bodies in the previous war and insisted that true faithfulness to Jesus Christ required total obedience to the Scriptures—including those commands not to resist an evildoer in Matt 5.[48] According to Althouse, Gee was "the most influential pacifist in Canada," as a conscientious objector during the First World War who admonished his fellow Pentecostals to beware of patriotic zeal.[49] In contrast to the overwhelming sentiment within the British Empire during the war that God was indeed on their side and that their efforts were a defense of Christian values, Gee charges that:

> However passionately patriotism may overwhelm everything else in time of war, the world certainly expects the Christian church to take a stand against war and it is deeply disappointed at heart when that stand is not taken . . . It would be exceedingly difficult for Britain or Germany, France or the United States, or any other nation to justify any claim to the express command and blessing of God, after such claims are made in time of war by contending armies.[50]

Note here that part of Gee's argument is rooted in the notion that even "the world," which Pentecostals often looked upon with disdain, expected the church to retain its pure witness against such atrocities, reinforcing the countercultural mindset that Pentecostalism retained into the 1930s. It is also apparent why early Pentecostals were so keen to keep this international movement from becoming entangled with the kingdoms of the world; in the same 1930 publication in which Gee published this article, another section documents the spread of the gospel across

---

48. Gee, "War, the Bible, and the Christian," 6–7.
49. Gee, "Conscientious Objection," 10.
50. Gee, "War, the Bible, and the Christian," 6–7.

such diverse lands as Peru, China, Japan, and Syria,[51] an emphasis which was typical of Pentecostal publications during the interwar period. That the pacifist sentiment remained strong throughout the interwar period is also demonstrated in denominational publications addressing the rise of fascism in Europe. Although Pentecostals were aware of the possibility of another major conflict, far from encouraging their readers to prepare for war as a patriotic duty, they perceived it as a sign of the times that ought to make believers long for the return of Christ. In response to Italian dictator Benito Mussolini's claim that fascism would overtake Europe within the decade, a 1933 edition of *The Pentecostal Evangel* declared that, "The eyes of many may be Romeward for their deliverer and the Antichrist may come from Rome; but the eyes of the saints will be heavenward, for we are looking for our Lord Jesus Christ to descend from heaven."[52] The discussion within the PAOC led George Chambers, the first General Superintendent of the denomination, to publish a series of articles in *The Pentecostal Testimony* beginning in November 1935 arguing vehemently that Christians ought not to participate in war,[53] a stance that should perhaps not be surprising given his Mennonite upbringing.[54] In his view, there was no more appropriate occasion for the disciples of Christ to act in armed defense of another than at Christ's arrest; yet, when Peter does so, the Lord rebukes him. Chambers asserts:

> It follows then, that if the disciples of the Lord were not given His permission to use the sword to fight for him, they were not to use it to fight for his interests, nor for the lesser purposes for which nations go to war today. If He did not want His followers to fight for Him when

---

51. "The Gospel in Foreign," *The Pentecostal Evangel*, 8 November 1930, 10–11. This section on international missions was a regular feature in the Assemblies of God's denominational publication.
52. "Will Anti-Christ," *The Pentecostal Evangel*, 4 February 1933, 5.
53. Chambers, "Should Christians Go," 13–14.
54. Ambrose, "On the Edge," 220–21.

He was about to be killed, by His enemies, does He want you and me to fight for the lesser things for which nations go to war?[55]

The implied answer to this rhetorical question is a resounding "no." He was not alone in addressing this topic; Linda Ambrose notes that articles in the PAOC publication which granted that "war was inevitable" and taking "a decidedly apocalyptic view" were not uncommon in the interwar period. Walter E. McAlister, another influential individual during the interwar years who would later go on to become General Superintendent himself, declared in a 1933 edition of *The Pentecostal Testimony* that the current Russian military buildup would lead the world toward the destruction outlined in Ezek 38, and predicted a worldwide war in the near future triggered by severe famine.[56] Nevertheless, in the same way that the American *Evangel* encouraged its readers to view conflict and tension as signs of the near return of Christ, such articles in *The Pentecostal Testimony* were quick to assert the same—and encouraged believers to demonstrate their readiness by preaching the gospel. One searches in vain for patriotic sentiment in 1930s Canadian Pentecostal newsletters, despite how often the possibility of conflict is highlighted.

It must also be noted that the sustained opposition to Christian participation in war during these two decades was not rooted in some naïve outlook that believed the First World War was, indeed "a war to end war"—a notion that Gee essentially ridicules in his aforementioned article.[57] On the contrary, particularly in the mid to late thirties, Pentecostal publications increasingly discussed the inevitability of war and the destruction it would again visit upon the world.[58] When Gee penned an article in *The Pentecostal Testimony* following an October 1934 visit to Germany, he applauded the "conscientious objectors among the Lutheran

---

55. Chambers, "Should Christians Go," 14.
56. McAlister, "Heralds of the King's," 5.
57. Gee, "War, the Bible, and the Christian," 6.
58. See, for example, Klinck, "War," 15. This particular publication, was aimed at youth, included a lengthy description of the new weapons that would be available for use in the next war, and declared that such a catastrophe was about to take place in Europe.

pastors" as one of the few obstacles to Adolf Hitler asserting total control over the nation.[59] A 1936 edition of *Christ's Ambassador's Herald* contained a brief biography of the *Fuhrer*, decrying his anti-Semitism, his disregard for the Versailles Treaty, and calling on believers to pray for the Jewish people and speak out against their oppression.[60] Yet, there is not a hint of militaristic sentiment; in fact, in the following month's edition of the same publication, the Roman Catholic Church is blasted on account of its half-hearted calls for peace and accused of actually aiding Benito Mussolini in his invasion of Ethiopia.[61]

Furthermore, while some such as Gee cautioned against hastily identifying Europe's fascist tyrants with the Antichrist,[62] other contributors to *The Pentecostal Testimony* labeled Mussolini a "modern Caesar" and were convinced that the prophecies recorded in Dan 11 were unfolding before their very eyes.[63] One looks in vain for any reference to Pentecostals preparing for war, even when references to the nations of the world doing so fill their publications. It seems that in the minds of many, the growing tensions in Europe served as a reminder that believers were not of the world—and that their hope of redemption was drawing near. However, as the situation intensified and the Second World War became all but inevitable, some Pentecostals in Canada began to adopt a more nuanced position on the question of military service—marking the start of an identity crisis of sorts for the relatively young movement.

World War II: Pacifism and Conscience

Twenty-five years after the outbreak of the First World War, the Pentecostal churches in Canada were no longer an informal collection of congregations with no centralized voice. Like their American counterparts, the PAOC reaffirmed its own position on

59. Gee, "The Truth about Hitler," 1–2.
60. Klinck, "Who is this Hitler," 4–5.
61. Klinck, "The Vatican," 16.
62. Gee, "The Truth about Hitler," 1.
63. Turvey, "Will Egypt Be Next?," 8–9.

conscientious objection in 1939.[64] Their statement built its argument on the authority of Scripture, which, as Pentecostals understood it, forbade believers from "shedding blood or taking human life." Once again appealing to New Testament texts that forbid acts of violence and/or murder by followers of Christ, Pentecostal leaders such as Gee argued forcefully that Christians should not be overtaken by patriotism. In his article for *The Pentecostal Testimony* concerning conscientious objection, he outlines five principles that ought to guide those who object to military service. Gee submits that conscientious objectors must refuse service on the basis of moral conviction, not fear of death or injury, nor may believers be involved in arms manufacturing while refusing to serve. He stipulates that the decision must not be based on political concerns and that to protect the witness of the church, conscientious objectors must not appear to be fanatics.[65] In short, his is a challenge against hypocrisy and inconsistency; if one refuses to serve, it must be on moral, not pragmatic, grounds. However, is it noteworthy that Gee's article, unlike earlier denominational resolutions and even his own writings, appears to present pacifism as a matter of conscience rather than a moral imperative. Like the PAOC's statement on conscientious objection, Gee does not flatly condemn military service, and the very fact that, in his view, one should object to service only if regulated by certain principles implies the possibility that one may find it consistent with their "principles" to serve in some capacity. While readers may still be tempted to read Gee's article and the PAOC statement as resolutely pacifist, they are remarkably tame when compared with the Assemblies of God official statement on the war. As Althouse notes, while the Canadian statement only affirms the movement's opposition to taking life, the American one rules out military service altogether—perhaps not surprisingly given that this precedent had already been established with the reaction to the First World War.[66] While this

---

64. Shuman, "Pentecost and the End," 75.
65. Gee, "Conscientious Objection," 10.
66. Althouse, "Canadian Pentecostal Pacifism," 33–34. The author does note that despite subtle differences, neither statement is "anti-state" and both, at

could reflect an adjustment due to context—readers of the Canadian publication, after all, would likely have not been as staunchly pacifist as those of the American *Evangel*—Gee's apparent subtle shift away from strict pacifism in such a short time may well serve as a microcosm of the movement at large. Despite the widespread attitude of conscientious objection that still typified Canadian Pentecostalism at the commencement of the war, it is also crucial to note that it was over the course of this conflict that the attitude of many adherents of the movement began to shift from this position and toward a more neutral—or just war—posture. One of the clearest indicators of change within the denomination may be viewed in *The Pentecostal Testimony*, the same publication which printed Gee's letter outlining principles for conscientious objection, which began to publish letters from Pentecostals in the military. Not only did the testimonies about evangelistic opportunities from these service members add a spiritual element to the conflict, but they eventually helped spread knowledge of the horrific actions of the Axis powers.[67] In an even more blatant turn away from the movement's early pacifism, *The Pentecostal Testimony* published the sermon of a British preacher in its January 1941 edition replete with nationalistic sentiment, declaring that the English speaking peoples of the world, "are destined to be His witnesses to the ungodly nations" and that they were "custodians of God's eternal truth."[68] Not only does the appearance of such statements in a Canadian publication prove that British imperialism remained alive and well in the dominion at this time, but also that its influence was beginning to outweigh that of the movement's earlier conviction concerning war. The editor of the paper, D. N. Buntain, concluded concerning military service in one 1939 edition that:

> It is not for any church or individual to dictate at this time, but to leave every individual to be guided by the Word of God and his own conscience. Let every man go to his knees and his Bible and be

least in theory, do leave open the possibility of non-combat roles in the military.
    67. Althouse, "Canadian Pentecostal Pacifism," 38–39.
    68. Morgan, "What is Britain's Destiny?," 12.

honest and true . . . If the call of the Empire becomes so insistent that he must decide, there are non-combatant units as the production units, the transport units, the hospital units, etc., where he can offer himself. On the other hand, if the believer feels that he should enlist in the standing army in any capacity, let the church keep silent. Let each person be guided in their own soul.[69]

Thus, if the witness of the denominational publication indicates anything, the war clearly marked a move from straightforward objection to a place of neutrality whereby military service was viewed as a matter of conscience. It also highlights a degree of tension within the movement's leadership. How could the editor of such a publication make this statement in the same general time frame that his denomination released a statement declaring themselves to be objectors? Newsletters such as *The Pentecostal Testimony* are particularly noteworthy in that they not only seem to push back against the established consensus early on in the war but also printed testimonies and columns during the war that implicitly highlighted some of the potential benefits of its adherents serving in the military. Celebrating the opportunities for evangelism that were presented in the armed forces, their newsletters highlight yet another possible catalyst for the decline in pacifism among Canadian Pentecostals: the primacy of missions. Pentecostalism has, from its infancy, emphasized evangelism more so than pacifism. Therefore, it appears that when military service came to be viewed as an evangelistic opportunity, reaching the lost took primacy over the commitment to nonviolence. As Althouse notes, many came to see the conflict as a means by which God could use his people to reach the world, further explaining that:

> Pentecostal pacifism declined for theological and sociological reasons. Pentecostals have always had a strong emphasis on missions. Moreover, pacifism was always second to missions and charismata . . . . with a military mission endeavor involving Pentecostals in the

---

69. Buntain, "The Pentecostal Movement," 3, cited in Dempster, "The Canada—Britain–USA," 14.

armed forces, the army became a mission field. Since then, more Pentecostals have entered the military with the intent to proselytize.[70]

What might be summarized, then, is that Pentecostals shifted away from their pacifist roots in no small part due to the logical implication, as they saw it, of even deeper concerns within their movement. Though pacifism may have been integral enough for the 1928 General Conference to include it in their *Statement of Fundamental and Essential Truths,* it simply was not the movement's *raison d'etre* in the way that missions clearly was.

A case in point on this topic can be observed in the case of bible college students. Unsurprisingly, military service proved to be a vital topic of conversation among college students at the time,[71] with Western Bible College in Winnipeg as a flashpoint for controversy. Along with the war came the conscription of young men, including students of the College; Reverend J. E. Purdie, then the college's principal, lobbied his PAOC colleagues to join him in fighting for his students to be allowed to remain in school after one had been drafted.[72] Neither he nor the student in question was a pacifist;[73] quite the contrary, he expressed full support for the allied powers, and referred to Hitler's ideology as demonic.[74] Rather, Purdie was concerned that his conscription would mean the loss of a promising minister to proclaim the soon return of Christ, which Purdie viewed as a higher obligation; his focus was on an eschatological vision, not cultural engagement. Hoping that Pentecostalism would no longer be seen as a fringe movement, but rather in the same category as the Catholics or other Protestants, when Purdie made the case to Canadian authorities that his students ought to be given exemption from service[75] he argued that doing so would allow them to train chaplains for the military. Yet, Pentecostals' ability to provide chaplaincy services was deemed negligible; even with the

70. Althouse, "Canadian Pentecostal Pacifism," 38–39.
71. Ambrose, "On the Edge," 215.
72. Ambrose, "On the Edge," 218.
73. See Ambrose, "On the Edge," 218.
74. Ambrose, "On the Edge," 222.
75. Ambrose, "On the Edge," 226.

changes that began to take place very few adherents served. Thus, it should not be shocking that Purdie found little favor with the authorities of the time. What is surprising, however, is Purdie also did not find strong support in the denomination as he almost certainly would have had in the First World War had he tried to find a means by which his students might avoid armed combat.

The 1941 General Superintendent D. N. Buntain—formerly the editor of *The Pentecostal Testimony*—took a more nuanced approach to the issue than his predecessor, George Chambers, who was a former Mennonite and staunch pacifist.[76] Assuming a posture that would likely have been anathema to Chambers, Buntain contended that young Pentecostals conscripts could use the occasion to spread the gospel. While not condemning conscientious objection, his stance is a marked change from that of Chambers. Moreover, in a 1945 correspondence between then General Superintendent, C. M. Wortman, and Reverend W. J. Taylor concerning the ordination of military-aged men, Wortman notably does not make any statement indicating Pentecostal men should not serve—implicitly treating it as a matter of conscience, not a matter on which to impose a blanket standard.[77] On the contrary, he states that he would not want to appeal for a military exemption for Pentecostal students training for ministry. It appears that, in a sense, the very thing that had prompted many first-generation Pentecostals to refuse military service ended up being the thing that pushed some in the next generation to allow it: a belief in the imminent return of Christ, and the consequential need for spreading the gospel. Though ironic, this view gained considerable traction over the course of the war.

The End of The War, The End of a Distinctive?

Just as the movement in Canada was more tempered in its pacifism early on than in the United States, so too the Canadian shift away from this position was quite subtle and gradual. That said,

---

76. Ambrose, "On the Edge," 221.
77. Wortman, "Christian Greetings."

it would be difficult to argue against the position that the Second World War proved to be a notable turning point based on PAOC literature. Perhaps the shift was inevitable; as the denomination grew and attracted converts from various Christian backgrounds, such individuals were bound to bring with them their own assumptions regarding war.[78] By the 1940s, when the denomination's attitude toward the subject began to shift, adherents included former Presbyterians, Anglicans, and others who were drawn to the more central doctrines of Pentecostalism, such as Spirit baptism, than to the finer distinctives of the movement like nonviolence.[79] It is not too surprising, then, that the relatively more peripheral teaching of pacifism faded into the background—especially when the influx of such converts from denominations with non-pacifist positions on war coincided with a major global crisis.

However, there could be an even deeper reason. While some Pentecostal scholars like Shuman see nonviolence as the proper scriptural response to war and advocate a return to it, Canadian scholar Peter Althouse argues that part of the reason that Pentecostals in his country moved away from pacifism is that the New Testament nowhere explicitly prohibits military participation.[80] While first-generation Pentecostals by and large took the New Testament's prohibition of killing as a prohibition of armed combat, the Bible also calls on believers to obey the governing authorities. Althouse, then, labels "inevitable" the emergence of a Pentecostal debate concerning whether war and killing were in fact the same thing—with many answering in the negative, thereby justifying military service.[81] Moreover, while early

---

78. Ambrose, "On the Edge," 219.
79. See Ambrose, "On the Edge," 219–20. The author notes "Diversity continued to be a defining feature of the movement and in 1943 Principal Purdie pointed out that the students who had studied at Western Bible College came from over 25 different countries and at least 23 different church backgrounds including Mennonite, Catholic, Baptist, Holiness Movement, and many more."
80. Althouse, "Canadian Pentecostal Pacifism," 40–41.
81. Allin, "Christianity and War," 4, cited in Althouse, "Canadian Pentecostal Pacifism," 40.

Pentecostals wished to avoid entanglement in the affairs of the world and thereby adopted a position of conscientious objection, during the Second World War it became clear that to object to military service was actually a far more politically charged stance than simply remaining neutral.[82] To openly criticize military involvement in the war was to "jeopardize the universal, Pentecostal message" by making it appear politically charged, whether this was the intent or not. In short, while the reasons for this shift in stance are multiple, and indeed quite complex, what seems clear is the movement's initial pacifist conviction proved no match when in conflict with the Pentecostal zeal for evangelism. Ultimately, this zeal helped bring members from virtually every Christian tradition into the Pentecostal fold including individuals who did not share their position on conscientious objection and thus, contributed to this notable change in the movement's outlook.

Bibliography

Alexander, Paul N., ed. *Pentecostals and Nonviolence: Reclaiming a Heritage*. Pentecostals, Peacemaking, and Social Justice 5. Eugene, OR: Pickwick, 2012.

Allin, A. E. "Christianity and War." *The Pentecostal Testimony* 21 (July 1940) 4.

Althouse, Peter. "Canadian Pentecostal Pacifism." *Eastern Journal of Practical Theology* 4 (1990) 32–43.

Ambrose, Linda M. "On the Edge of War and Society: Canadian Pentecostal Bible School Students in the 1940s." *Journal of the Canadian Historical Association* 24 (2013) 215–47.

Bartleman, Frank. "Christian Citizenship." Los Angeles: [n.p.], 1922.

---

82. Althouse, "Canadian Pentecostal Pacifism," 41.

———. "War and the Christian." *Word and Work* (1915) 4–5.

Beaman, Jay. *Pentecostal Pacifism: The Origin, Development, and Rejection of Pacific Belief among the Pentecostals*. Eugene, OR: Wipf & Stock, 2009.

Berger, Carl. *The Sense of Power: Studies in the Ideas of Canadian Imperialism, 1867–1914*. 3rd ed. Toronto: University of Toronto Press, 2013.

Buntain, E. N. "The Pentecostal Movement and War." *The Pentecostal Testimony* (2 October 1939) 3.

Canada Department of Justice, "Military Service Act, 1917: Important Notice." Acts of the Parliament of Canada 1917 (May 1918). https://www.torontopubliclibrary.ca/detail.jsp?R=DC-1918ACTVS.

Canadian Pentecostal Testimony. "The Paper." December 1920.

Chambers, G. A. *50 Years in the Service of the King, 1907–1957*. Toronto: Full Gospel, 1960.

———. "Should Christians Go to War?" *The Pentecostal Testimony* (November 1935) 14.

"Combined Minutes of the General Council of the Assemblies of God, Held at Hot Springs, Arkansas, April 2–12, 1914." Findlay, OH: Gospel Publishing House, 1914.

Combined Minutes of the General Council of The Assemblies of God. St. Louis: [n.p.], 1916.

Crouse, Eric. "Canada's Salvation Army and the War: The War Cry, Soul Saving, and the South African War." In *Empire from the Margins: Religious Minorities in Canada and the South African War*, edited by Gordon L. Heath, 85–99.

McMaster General Studies Series 11. Eugene, OR: Pickwick, 2017.

Davidson, Melissa. "The Anglican Church and the Great War." In *Canadian Churches and the First World War*, edited by Gordon L. Heath, 152–69. McMaster General Series 4. Eugene, OR: Pickwick, 2014.

Dayton, Donald W. *An Historical Survey of Attitudes Toward War and Peace Within the American Holiness Movement*. Winona Lake, IN: The Seminar, 1973.

Dempster, Murray W. "The Canada—Britain—USA Triad: Canadian Pentecostal Pacifism in WWI and WWII." *Canadian Journal of Pentecostal-Charismatic Christianity* 4 (2013) 1–26.

———. "'Crossing Borders': Arguments Used by Early American Pentecostals in Support of the Global Character of Pacifism." *Journal of the European Pentecostal Theological Association* 10.2 (1991) 63–80.

Gee, Donald. "Conscientious Objection." *The Pentecostal Testimony* 1 (15 February 1940) 10.

———. "The Truth About Hitler and Germany." *The Pentecostal Testimony* 2 (February 1935) 1–2.

———. "War, the Bible, and the Christian." *The Pentecostal Evangel* (8 November 1930) 6–7.

Hauerwas, Stanley. "Foreword." In *Pentecostals and Nonviolence: Reclaiming a Heritage*, edited by Paul N. Alexander, xiii–xv. Pentecostals, Peacemaking, and Social Justice 5. Eugene, OR: Pickwick, 2012.

Haykin, Michael A. G., and Ian Hugh Clary. "'O God of Battles': The Canadian Baptist Experience of the Great

War." In *Canadian Churches and the First World War*, edited by Gordon L. Heath, 170–96. McMaster General Series 4. Eugene, OR: Pickwick, 2014.

Heath, Gordon L. "American Churches and the First World War: An Introduction." In *American Churches and the First World War*, edited by Gordon L. Heath, 1–14. McMaster Divinity College General Series 7. Eugene, OR: Pickwick, 2016.

———. "Canadian Churches and War: An Introductory Essay and Annotated Bibliography." *McMaster Journal of Theology and Ministry* 12 (2010–2011) 61–124.

Klinck, Otto J. "The Vatican and The Sword." *Christ's Ambassadors Herald* 9.6 (June 1936) 16.

———. "War." *Christ's Ambassadors Herald* 9.11 (November 1935) 15.

———. "Who is this Hitler Who Defies the World?" *Christ's Ambassadors Herald* 9 (May 1936) 4–5.

McAlister, Walter E. "Heralds of the King's Return." *The Pentecostal Testimony* 5 (June 1933) 5.

McCutcheon, M. F., et al. *The Christian and War: An Appeal*. Toronto: McClelland & Stewart, 1926.

Miller, Carman. "Writing Religious Minorities into Canada's South African War, 1899–1902." In *Empire from the Margins: Religious Minorities in Canada and the South African War*, edited by Gordon L. Heath, 16–35. McMaster General Studies Series 11. Eugene, OR: Pickwick, 2017.

Miller, Thomas William. *Canadian Pentecostals: A History of the Pentecostal Assemblies of Canada*. Mississauga, ON: Full Gospel, 1994.

"Minutes of the Pentecostal Assemblies of Canada." November 25–28, 1919. The Pentecostal Assemblies of Canada Archives, Mississauga, ON, Canada.

Morgan, J. J. "What is Britain's Destiny?" *The Pentecostal Testimony* (January 1941) 12.

The Pentecostal Evangel. "The Gospel in Foreign Lands." 8 November 1930.

———. "Will Anti-Christ Rise in Rome?" 4 February 1933.

The Pentecostal Testimony. "A Statement of Fundamental Truths Approved by the Pentecostal Assemblies of Canada." (October 1928).

Penton, M. James. "Wells, David." In *Dictionary of Canadian Biography*. Vol. 14. Toronto: University of Toronto/ Université Laval, 2003, http://www.biographi.ca/en/bio/wells_david_14E.html.

Robeck, Cecil M. Jr. "Bartleman, Frank." In *The New International Dictionary of Pentecostal and Charismatic Movements*, edited by Stanley M. Burgess, 366. Rev. ed. Grand Rapids: Zondervan, 2002.

Shuman, Joel. "Pentecost and the End of Patriotism: A Call for The Restoration of Pacifism Among Pentecostal Christians." *Journal of Pentecostal Theology* 4 (1996) 70–96.

Socknat, Thomas. "Conscientious Objectors in the Context of Canadian Peace Movements." *Journal of Mennonite Studies* 25 (2007) 61–74.

Turvey, A. J. "Will Egypt Be Next?" *The Pentecostal Testimony* (June 1936) 8–9.

Wacker, Grant. *Heaven Below: Early Pentecostals and American Culture*. Cambridge, MA: Harvard University Press, 2015.

Wortman, C. M. "Christian Greetings." Letter to Rev. W. J. Taylor. March 22, 1945. The Pentecostal Assemblies of Canada Archives, Mississauga, ON, Canada.

Yoder, John Howard. *Christian Attitudes to War, Peace, and Revolution*, edited by Ted Koontz and Andy Alexis-Baker. Grand Rapids: Brazos, 2009.

Mobile Killing Units, Lopuchowa Forest, Poland

Jill Peláez Baumgaertner[1]
Chicago, IL, USA

The hush in the forest is calming at first
and then not. No songs to sing along this via dolorosa
except Kaddish. I walk on pine needles decades
after thousands were herded like animals to the pit
that is just ahead. The silent whispers of the dead

linger, caught even in the branches of these straight
pines, still sloughing, still seeping into the soil.
Yes, Baumgartner is written in the death
roles at Auschwitz, Peláez in the archive
of victims and survivors, but this is not my story,

each name a blood line, each silenced voice words
unlinked from mine. This is not my story, yet I,
a Jew of the New Testament, am stumbling along,
my year-old child clinging to my neck.
For a flash of a second I am aware of one sharp
breath and the beginning of a fall into the abyss.

This is not my story, I keep repeating.
This is not my story.

---

1. Jill Peláez Baumgaertner is Poetry Editor for *The Christian Century* and served as Dean of Humanities and Theological Studies at Wheaton College from 2001–2017 and Acting Provost from 2017–18.

SCIANA PLACZU

Jill Peláez Baumgaertner
Chicago, IL, USA

Kazimierz, Poland

The Jewish headstones broken under Nazi tanks,
the annihilation so complete even death's work
crushed, the testament of lives obliterated.

These headstones now puzzle-pieced to form
a thirty-foot wall, each stone, each fragment
with their menorahs, candles, pitchers, broken

branches, a person in each symbol, a name.
A jagged slash, like lightning, from ground
to full height, dark with shadow like a rent

garment, wide enough to step through
into another world of mist and pine-needled
floor, the forest filtering daylight like looking

through the sheerest organdy, a place to stand
with beauty, a place to stand with beauty
ripped apart like the curtain of the temple
torn in two.

CONCENTRATION

Jill Peláez Baumgaertner
Chicago, IL, USA

"... In this connection, it is to be borne in mind that only cities which are rail junctions, or at least are located along railroad lines, are to be designated as concentration points."—Heydrich's Instructions to Chiefs of Einsatzgruppen, September 21, 1939[2]

"The area of the camp is so small that, had the new arrivals stayed alive for even a few days, it would have been only a week and a half before there was no more space behind the barbed wire for this tide of people flowing in from Poland, from Belorussia, from the whole of Europe."—Vasily Grossman, 1944[3]

The word itself:
to focus
to compress
to remove all
distractions
to create less and less
space
for interruption
to fill the smaller
and smaller
spaces with
more and more.

The word
becomes sinister.

2. Cited in Dawidowicz, ed., *A Holocaust Reader*, 60.
3. Cited in "Excerpts from 'The Hell of Treblinka,'" [n.p.].

To cut even
that space in half
to cut the half
space by two-thirds.

Packed
into stinking rooms
and then transported
crushed standing
in boxcars
6000 a day
Treblinka.

The camp map:
storehouse for victims'
property
disguised as a train station
execution site
disguised as hospital
barracks where women
undressed
had heads shaved
barracks where men undressed
"the Tube"—the path
to the gas chambers
three old
ten new gas chambers
the cremation pyres.

Today we walk
the forest path
now level ground
the forest path
the forest path
then the clearing
and the ragged stones
standing, these stones
a compression

a concentration
of heat and pressure
pushed
by the earth's crust
from its core
the stones
the rocks
spaced in the clearing
lined up
a congregation
of what's left
after suffering
nothing but jagged
edges,
the silence
its own Golgotha.

Bibliography

Dawidowicz, Lucy S., ed. *A Holocaust Reader*. Library of Jewish Studies. West Orange, NJ: Behrman House, 1976.

Facing History and Ourselves. "Excerpts from 'The Hell of Treblinka' by Vasily Grossman, 1944." Online: https://www.facinghistory.org/holocaust-human-behavior/hell-of-treblinka-vasily-grossman

THE RELATIONSHIP BETWEEN WORK AND WEALTH IN
PROVERBS: A STUDY OF TWO "CONTRADICTORY"
SAYINGS (PROVERBS 14:23 AND 23:4–5)

Kojo Okyere
University of Cape Coast, Cape Coast, Ghana

Readers of the book of Proverbs are confronted with what appears to be contradictory sayings.[1] When readers perceive proverbial sayings to be contradictory, the didactic function of the sayings, and by extension the book, is called into question. Scholars have varied reactions toward these contradictions,[2] either explaining them away and insisting they are not contradictions or affirming the presence of contradictions while offering explanations that point to their value. Claudia Camp, for instance, argues that the presence of contradictions is indicative of

---

1. By contradictory sayings, I refer to sayings that give opposing or conflicting meanings, lessons, or values. Such sayings appear to be inconsistent with each other. Proverbs 26:4–5, which juxtaposes two opposing views on how one should relate to a fool, serves as an example. There are also subtle contradictions, such as the advice on bribery in Prov 21:14 and 17:23.

2. The book of Proverbs is not the only proverbial material containing contradictions that has drawn the attention of scholars. Scholars in the field of paremiology and folklore studies have sought to address the issue. Yankah, "Do Proverbs Contradict?" 2–9, for instance, contends that proverbs do not contradict each other if placed in context. He explains that the problem of contradictory proverbs arises only because people fail to situate proverbs within a performance context. Mieder, *Proverbs*, 133–34, concurs with Yankah that there is no doubt that when one takes proverbs outside their performance context, they may contradict each other. However, in the performance context, contradictions serve as strategies by the users. He concludes that "Proverbs in normal discourse are not contradictory at all, and they usually make perfect sense to the speaker and listener."

the dynamic social and moral world behind the sayings. These contradictions have a pedagogical value, especially in the construction of the moral self.[3] Other scholars insist, rather, that the contradictions should be seen as complementary.[4] Zoltán Schwáb contends that putting the contradictory sayings in clusters reveals their complementarity. Arguing from what he calls an associative strategy, he explains that what appears as a contradiction may be complementary, especially when interpreters are willing to be guided by dominating themes within clusters.[5] Prior to Schwáb's argument, Peter Hatton made a case for rejecting the idea of contradictions in Proverbs.[6] Unlike Schwáb, who uses clusters of sayings to argue for complementary reading, Hatton argues that complementary reading is possible for the entire book of Proverbs. He rejects early scholarship that presented Proverbs as atomistic collections and calls for a deeper appreciation of the carefully crafted and skillfully organized composition of the book. His position can be summed up in his words; "contradictions in the book are intrinsic to its purpose and not accidental."[7]

3. Camp, "Proverbs and the Moral Self," 25–42. See also Collins, *Introduction to the Hebrew Bible*, 493, who attributes the problem of contradictions to the tension between pragmatism and idealism. For Collins, on the one hand, the sayings have a practical purpose in guiding young ones to making the best decisions for life. On the other hand, some of the sayings aim at very high standards, and in the process, they become tendentious and unrealistic. Also see, Yodder, "Forming 'Fearers of Yahweh,'" 167–84 and Dell, *The Book of Proverbs*, 54.

4. This proposal represents a relatively new stage in the studies of Proverbs where the book is no longer perceived to be a haphazard collection of sayings. Early modern studies on Proverbs downplayed the book's value due to the understanding that Proverbs contained sayings, which were for the most part randomly organized resulting in paradoxes and contradictions. Toy, *Book of Proverbs*, *viii*, for instance, describes the book as lacking logical arrangement, a characteristic of the book that creates difficulty in one's attempt to create some form of structure (apart from the divisions already in the book).

5. Schwáb, "The Sayings Clusters in Proverbs," 59–79.
6. Hatton, *Contradictions in the Book of Proverbs*.
7. Hatton, *Contradictions in the Book of Proverbs*, 11.

Inspired by Hatton's thesis, this paper argues that although there are apparent contradictions in Proverbs, especially within proverbial sayings on the relationship between wealth and work, close attention to the rhetoric of these sayings in light of sociological and theoretical insights about work reveals elements of complementarity.[8] Using Prov 14:23 and 23:4–5 as a case study, I explore how perceived contradictions between sayings on work and wealth can be explained in a manner that avoids compromising the didactic value of the sayings.[9] To achieve this goal, I first carry out an exegesis of the two texts to reveal their message. Next, I explore what may give rise to contradictions within the selected sayings. I then resolve the apparent contradictions by appealing to the nature of the sayings and the theory of work values.

Exegesis of Proverbs 14:23 and 23:4–5

A series of headings divides Proverbs into seven collections.[10] These two texts fall within the second and third sections. Proverbs 14:23 is part of the second collection (Prov 10:1—22:16)

8. In a similar discussion, Van Leeuwen, in "Wealth and Poverty," 34–35, wrestles with the issue of contradictions. He explains that contradictions "reveal basic conflicts within a worldview" (25) and as a result, function paradigmatically. Emanating from the reality of life, these contradictions call for deeper engagement with the texts with respect to the dynamics of the possibilities produced by the encounter between faith and life.
9. The selected texts fall under different collections within Proverbs. While this may seem a haphazard selection, it should rather be construed as a purposeful choice, one based on a conviction that many readers (especially ordinary readers) approach the book as a unit. Also, as Hatton argues, the book's structure is such that a saying in one collection may throw light on other sayings in the same or in a different collection. For him, the book is a unified text in which the sayings interact with each other irrespective of their location. See Hatton, *Contradictions in the Book of Proverbs*, 4.
10. Using the headings, seven main collections or divisions emerge. However, other variables such as the type of saying and the direction of the sayings can lead to further divisions of the book. See Waltke, *The Book of Proverbs*, 9; also cf. Fox, *Proverbs 1–9*, 4.

known as the Solomonic Sayings. As the largest collection in Proverbs, it sets itself apart from the preceding and proceeding collections mainly due to the form of its sayings. Short and pithy sayings which come in two-part lines or sentences characterize most of the proverbs. They are referred to as aphorisms or sentence literature.[11] Two main subdivisions have been identified: chs. 10–15 and 16:1—22:16. In the former, most of the sayings have parallel lines that contrast; while in the latter, the second line affirms, extends, or exemplifies what the first line says.

Proverbs 23:4–5 is part of the collection titled the Words of the Wise (Prov. 22:17—24:22). This collection has a relationship with an Egyptian text called the Instructions of Amenemope, which is dated *circa* 1100 BCE.[12] The literary uniqueness of this collection is borne out of the fact that the sayings are longer than the sentence literature in the preceding collection. The use of imperatives and extended admonitions followed by motive clauses, however, makes them stand close to the lectures of Prov 1–9, although they are less expressive than those of Prov 1–9. Thirty sayings make up this collection and among the themes discussed are the good and wicked, the conduct of the youth, and wealth.

Text: Proverbs 14:23

בְּכָל־עֶצֶב יִהְיֶה מוֹתָר וּדְבַר־שְׂפָתַיִם אַךְ־לְמַחְסוֹר
In all labor there is profit; but mere talk surely leads to poverty.

---

11. See Waltke, *The Book of Proverbs*, 14.
12. Several scholars are of the view that there is a creative adaptation of the Egyptian text by the Hebrew text. See the following for exhaustive discussions on the relationship between the two works: Ruffle, "The Teaching of Amenemope," 29–68; Fox, "The Formation of Proverbs 22:17—23:11," 22–37; Fox, *Proverbs 10–31*, 753–67; and Clarke, "Wisdom Literature and the Question of Priority," 50–56. The studies by K. A. Kitchen are particularly insightful as he uses linguistic and stylistic parallels to argue not only for the independence of the biblical unit, but also for the Solomonic authorship of the unit of Prov 1–24. See Kitchen, "Proverbs and Wisdom Books of the Ancient Near East," 69–114, and "Basic Literary Forms and Formulations," 235–92.

OKYERE *Work and Wealth* 91

Proverbs 14:23 falls under the antithetical group of sayings (Prov 10–15). For Waltke, this saying is part of the unit formed in vv. 19–24, which contrasts "consequences of comportment using mostly ethical terms."[13] He further strikes a relationship between v. 23 and v. 24 on the conceptual level of their message. The wise and the fool of v. 24 are respectively connected to the wise and foolish acts of hard work and mere talk in v. 23.

As an antithetical couplet, Prov 14:23 focuses on two actions and their respective consequences. The first colon opens with the phrase "in all labor" (בְּכָל־עֶצֶב) which paints a picture of hard and painful work. Following is the copula verb "to be" (יִהְיֶה) which connects the preceding image of "labor" (עֶצֶב) to "profit/gain" (מוֹתָר). The choice of the noun עֶצֶב is deliberate. Conveying physical and emotional discomfort, עֶצֶב stresses the pain one goes through when working. According to Swanson, the verb עָצַב means "to hurt, grieve, or pain," and the noun form of the same root refers to "pain, toil, or hurt."[14] Our first encounter of the word in the Hebrew Bible is in Gen 3:16–17 during the pronouncement of Adam's and Eve's punishment. In Eve's situation, עֶצֶב projects both physical and emotional pain resulting from pregnancy and birth, and by extension the stress that comes with family conflicts. In Adam's case, the term refers to the difficulties of making a living.[15] A similar meaning emerges from the use of עֶצֶב in Ps 127:2, where the psalmist refers to the discomfort and agony associated with a long and arduous task.[16]

In the context of 14:23, the word conveys the discomfort associated with strenuous work. It is significant to note that the sage is emphatic in giving a positive evaluation of strenuous work through the qualification of עֶצֶב with the determiner כָּל

---

13. Waltke, *The Book of Proverbs*, 597.
14. Swanson, *Dictionary of Biblical Languages with Semantic Domains*, 6676, #3.
15. Westermann, *Genesis 1–11*, 261–62.
16. It is important to note how the themes of "toil" and "weariness" are picked up in Ecclesiastes. The Preacher views labor as one of the troubles of life. However, in Ecclesiastes, several terms, including עֶצֶב and תִּיגַע, are used to capture the enigma of life. More of this association is discussed in the conclusion.

(all). Waltke gives two possible usages of כֹּל: definite or indefinite qualification of עֶצֶב. If the former, כָּל refers to the "entirety" or "whole" of work; if the latter, then it refers to all kinds of work.[17] The point here is that despite the pain and discomfort that comes with strenuous work, there is an implied positive value placed on it. In the words of Fox, "Prov 14:23a is more sanguine about the value of hard work."[18] By using the verb יִהְיֶה to connect the subject and the complement, the sage emphasizes the relative truth of the claim that profit or gain and hard work go together.

Like the first, the second colon opens with the subject, "but mere talk" (וּדְבַר־שְׂפָתַיִם), which serves as a contrast to עֶצֶב. The phrase וּדְבַר־שְׂפָתַיִם can be translated literally as "but a thing/word of the lips." Its usage is metonymical. It stands for unproductive talk or failure to accomplish what is said (cf. 2 Kgs 20:18; Isa 36:5). In this regard, the sage contrasts hard work with mere talk or empty words. The concern is with people who do not follow through on their words. Such a lifestyle has its consequence: it leads to low productivity and then to the state of want. Accordingly, the concluding phrase of the second colon, "surely leads to poverty" (אַךְ־לְמַחְסוֹר), cautions against the fate of such an action. By opening the concluding phrase, the particle "surely" (אַךְ), highlights the expected conclusion of "poverty" (מַחְסוֹר). Alliteration is used to associate the words מַחְסוֹר and מוֹתָר, and connect them to their actions of mere talk and hard work respectively.

The thrust of the message in Prov 14:23 is that commitment to hard work leads to gain or some kind of benefit. On the contrary, verbosity and undirected conversation are a waste of time; they could cause a person to be poor. Antithesis is the main rhetorical strategy. Interestingly, the contrast is not between an action and inaction as observed in other sayings about work (cf. Prov 6:6–11; 10:4; 12:17; 20:13). Working hard and talking are both actions, but one leads to a gain while the other does not. The kind of action one engages in is therefore important.

17. Waltke, *The Book of Proverbs*, 601.
18. Fox, *Proverbs 10–31*, 523.

Engaging in an activity that leads to no productivity is an unwise act. The use and placement of the only verb (יִהְיֶה) in a construction entirely dominated by nouns is worth noting. Used mainly to emphasize the state of being, יִהְיֶה "signifies the universal truth that profit exists, is present, or is in the process of becoming and lying in the future."[19] It can be attained only through hard work. The message, suffer to gain, is a conviction that is common to many primitive societies. Such belief systems partly stem from the crude manner they engaged with their environment to make a living. An ancient Israelite agricultural context, which was characterized by low rainfall, heavy soil erosion, and desert-like lands, indicates the difficulty individuals had to go through in farming practices.[20]

Text: Proverbs 23:4–5

אַל־תִּיגַע לְהַעֲשִׁיר מִבִּינָתְךָ חֲדָל
Do not toil to be rich; from your own understanding cease.

הֲתָעִיף עֵינֶיךָ בּוֹ וְאֵינֶנּוּ
For when your eyes fly upon it, it is gone,

כִּי עָשֹׂה יַעֲשֶׂה־לּוֹ כְנָפַיִם כְּנֶשֶׁר יָעוּף הַשָּׁמָיִם
for it suddenly makes to itself wings; like an eagle and it flies to the sky.

As part of the collection titled the Words of the Wise (Prov 22:17—24:22), Prov 23:4–5 is the seventh saying within the collection and its makeup consists of a couplet and a tricolon. Verse 4, the couplet, opens with the negation אַל fixed to the jussive תִּיגַע to form the imperative[21] "do not toil." The Hebrew word

19. Waltke, *The Book of Proverbs*, 601.
20. Borowski, *Daily Life in Biblical Times*, 26–28.
21. My designation of this form as an imperative may be problematic as the designation itself suggests a particular grammatical form in Hebrew which is not equivalent to the "negative command" expressed by the negative adverb plus jussive. However, I am looking at the function of the form in this case.

תִּיגַע means to become weary by working.[22] It indicates the extra effort one puts into accomplishing a task (cf. Josh 7:3). It also points to perseverance as depicted in Job 9:29. Closing the first part of the colon is the word לְהַעֲשִׁיר which means "to be rich." By expressing concern about the extent to which one works, the sage puts into perspective the goals which may underpin one's work. In this particular instance, the concern is that working hard (in a way that wearies the body) to achieve the goal of creating wealth[23] may be unwise. The reason for this apprehension is developed in the tricolon of v. 5.

The second colon of v. 4 opens with the phrase "from your own understanding" (מִבִּינָתְךָ). Here, the sage alludes to the personal pain one encounters in a work that is continuous and toilsome. A wise person learns from his/her experiences. Thus, one's engagement in תִּיגַע should lead one to the "insight" (בִּינָה) of its potential dangers. The pronominal suffix "your" (ךָ) stresses the essence of self-reflection. For the sage, self-reflection on the unguarded pursuit of wealth is the issue. The *qal* imperative "cease" (חֲדָל) closes the second colon and negates a previously referred to action. Since the first verb, תִּיגַע, has already been negated, it is likely that חֲדָל points to בִּינָה. Although Fox agrees, he provides a nuanced meaning of the second colon translating the line as "Leave off your starring!"[24] He tries to avoid the confusion that arises from translating בִּינָה as "understanding." It is simply impossible for one to cease from using one's own understanding; this is always true even when מִבִּינָתְךָ חֲדָל is taken as "cease from" or "cease because of."[25]

---

22. Baker and Carpenter, *The Complete Word Study Dictionary*, 417.

23. The noun "wealth," עֹשֶׁר, is not stated explicitly in the text. It is implied in the construction לְהַעֲשִׁיר which can be translated "to be rich." See Fox, *Proverbs 10–31*, 723.

24. Fox, *Proverbs 10–31*, 723.

25. Although Fox's explanation is tenable, it is also true that those who render בִּינָה as "understanding" are constrained by the first colon which alludes to one's experiences. The sage may be concerned about the experiences one has accumulated over the years in toiling for

Verse 5 provides the reason for the sage's misgivings about toiling to become rich. The first colon begins the description of wealth's ephemeral character. The image, "when your eyes fly on it" (הֲתָעִיף עֵינֶיךָ), depicts wealth's attractive prowess.[26] "It" refers to wealth as implied in לְהַעֲשִׁיר of v. 4. But immediately as one gazes on wealth, it goes away (וְאֵינֶנּוּ). How does this happen? Wealth develops "wings" (כְנָפַיִם): it does so quickly and unexpectedly. This view is conveyed by the expression כִּי עָשֹׂה יַעֲשֶׂה־לֹּוֹ, "for suddenly it makes to itself," which is a construction that expresses certainty or emphasis. Thus, wealth will surely grow wings; this includes an element of suddenness. The last colon gives the destination for the flying wealth. Simile is used to liken wealth with an "eagle" (נֶשֶׁר). Thus, like an eagle, wealth takes to "the sky" (הַשָּׁמָיִם) beyond the reach of humans. Accordingly, the point is that one needs to be careful in the quest for riches since wealth can be unpredictable.

Proverbs 23:4–5 cautions against straining oneself to be rich. Such an approach to wealth sends the message that attaining wealth is solely dependent on one's effort; God plays little to no role. However, Proverbs offers a nuanced theology on the role God plays in human welfare. For instance, Prov 10:22 says that wealth comes from God's blessings. Fox gives a two-step interpretation of this saying. First, Prov 10:22 is a reminder to all who have wealth that God is the source of their riches. Second,

---

wealth. By pointing to בִּינָה, חֲדַל does not mean a total ban on the use of one's intelligence as Fox seems to suggest.

26. The reading of הֲתָעִיף follows the *qere*, although it does not appear elsewhere as a *hiphil*, but the *ketib* is difficult to render in its context. The entire expression הֲתָעִיף עֵינֶיךָ בּוֹ וְאֵינֶנּוּ, "for when your eyes fly upon it, it is gone," suggests covetousness on the part of the worker. If this suggestion is valid, then one of the concerns of the sage is the unguarded quest for wealth. Such an attitude can only lead to weariness of the body and deceit of the heart. Covetousness is rebellion against God. In Ps 10:3, for instance, a covetous person cuts God away from his life mainly because the things sought after replaces God in the heart. When a worker is motivated solely through the desire to amass wealth, such a person may never have satisfaction (cf. Eccl 5:10) as greed eats satisfaction and contentment out of one's heart. The security of wealth may turn out to be false (Prov 23:5).

human effort expended towards creating wealth has a limit.[27] The thinking that this limitation can be dealt with through excessive work is not only deceptive but also unwise. Thus, the use of the negative command "cease from your own understanding" appeals to individuals of such persuasions to reflect on the experience of creating wealth.

A Superficial Case of Contradiction

A superficial reading of the two sayings may lead to conflicting values. First, where and how do the contradictions, if any, emerge? Proverbs 14:23 claims that in all labor there is profit or gain. However, idle talk leads to poverty or states of want. Two correlations can be discerned: (1) labor leads to gain/profit; and (2) idle talk leads to poverty. On the other hand, 23:4–5 cautions against extraneous hard work for the purpose of gaining wealth. Two inferences can likewise be discerned: (1) do not engage in hard work to gain wealth; and (2) wealth is ephemeral/unreliable.

The two sayings display an apparent contradiction on the relationship between work and wealth, although they also seem to agree that work somehow leads to a gain. Particularly explicit in 14:23 is this latter claim. Positive and negative illustrations are used to drive home the claim that hard work guarantees a gain or profit. Negative illustration is the main strategy in Prov 23:4–5 as it states inversely what Prov 14:23 only hints at. By their diction (עֶצֶב and תִּיגַע), the sayings agree that work could be stressful, strenuous, and demanding; but it is this kind of activity that could lead one to a gain.

Despite their tacit agreement on the output of hard work, the two sayings may be construed as presenting conflicting inferences. First, they seem to differ regarding the significance placed on the output of work. While 14:23 appears to place a positive value on מוֹתָר (gain/profit), 23:4–5 places a caution on wealth when it characterizes it as ephemeral or untrustworthy. In 14:23, מוֹתָר prevents one from becoming poor. Hard work is promoted as a guarantee for success, one that could liberate the worker

---

27. Fox, *Proverbs 10–31*, 523.

from the shackles of poverty. Thus, מוֹתָר is a positive stimulus used by the sage to persuade the audience to continuously choose hard work over fruitless idle talk. This positive value on work's output (מוֹתָר) appears downplayed in 23:4–5. Wealth[28] assumes an ephemeral character. It is here today and absent tomorrow. It is unpredictable and therefore unreliable. Meanwhile, in 14:23, there is no hint of unpredictability on the part of מוֹתָר, which may include wealth. Rather, there is the assurance that one stands to gain from one's work. Interestingly, the wealth alluded to in 23:4–5, which is unpredictable, can be attained through one's labor just like in 14:23.

Second, there may be conflicting values on the place of labor in one's life. To put it simply, is it incumbent for individuals to engage in hard work? Proverbs 14:23 does not shy away from promoting hard work as a positive value. Opting for the verb עֶצֶב, the sage is conscious of the level of difficulty that such work entails, yet continues to give an overall positive evaluation of it. This overall positive evaluation of hard work is missing in Proverbs 23:4–5.[29] Pain and discomfort are to be avoided here, unlike 14:23 which embraces them as necessary for making a profit. The double negatives used in 23:4 are indicative of apprehension on the part of the sage towards work that wearies the body in order to attain wealth. This being the case, one wonders if there is any occasion where hard work (one that strains the body) can be justified in the eyes of the sage. Will he accept exhaustive labor directed at another goal besides creating wealth?[30]

---

28. In Prov 23:4–5, wealth emerges as the output of work.
29. However, it needs to be pointed out that the saying does not prohibit hard work altogether. Rather the sage discourages the audience from engaging in a work that makes the body weary just to become rich. In other words, the prohibition is qualified.
30. This is difficult to determine from the text, but I argue for the negative. What the text appears to communicate is that wearying the body for any outcome is unwise. I explain later that implied in the sage's rhetoric is the wisdom of optimizing one's energy to work, which is different from working exhaustively to attain an elusive goal.

Proverbs 14:23 and 23:4–5 as Complementary Sayings

A superficial reading of the two sayings may present conflicting values to readers. However, as Yankah[31] and Meider[32] argue, is it possible that the seeming contradictions are only prominent because the sayings appear in a collection? Could the contradictions disappear if the sayings were used in a performance context? Better still, can the contradictions be resolved if close attention is paid to the nature and goal of the sayings? This section appeals to the sociological theory of work values to demonstrate how the two sayings can be read as complementary. However, before that is done, let us explore how the nature of the sayings help to resolve the presence of contradictions.

A conspicuous contrast between the two sayings is the mode in which the message is communicated. While 14:23 is a declarative statement, 23:4–5 is couched in a dyadic structure of imperatives[33] and a declarative. In 14:23, the sage is stating an axiom: if work or labor is the exertion of force towards an end, then there is a guarantee of an output. Such conclusions have become self-evidently true within Israelite society. Undoubtedly, the sage has witnessed the strenuous effort Israelites put into their farming practices and the resulting output of their efforts. The narrator of Gen 3 presents the relationship between work and gain in a similar manner. In Gen 3:17, the Lord God pronounced a curse on the ground as a way of punishing man. This etiological story communicates the truth about difficulty in work (which was mainly agricultural). By employing a declarative statement, the sage of 14:23 only echoes the generally accepted truth that work leads to an output, which more often than not is a gain of some sort. A combination of an imperative and a declarative statement is used in 23:4–5. This indicates the presence of personal opinions interlaced with axioms or generally accepted truths. By using the declarative, 14:23 is generalized in its message. The double commands of 23:4 give specific injunctions. In this case, moving into the realm of the sage's personal belief on the

31. Yankah, "Do Proverbs Contradict?" 2–9.
32. Mieder, *Proverbs*, 133–34.
33. Refer to note 21.

relationship between wealth and work. Through the commands, a personal connection is made with the sage. Shifting to a declarative statement in v. 5, the sage gives the basis for his earlier conviction in v. 4. However, this time there is a shift from specifics to generalization. Thus, a case of complementarity can be seen in the functions of the sayings. The combination of declarative statements and imperatives functions to supply readers with information and at the same time caution them against a particular line of action. Both sayings provide the information that hard work leads to some outcome related to wealth. Through its imperatives, 23:4–5, however, goes further to caution against inordinate pursuit of wealth. Because of its transient and perishable character, wealth may not be a trusted motivation for work. The use of the negative commands places a serious tone on the counsel being given: apply wisdom when it comes to working hard for the purpose of creating wealth.[34]

Now, how can the theory of work values help readers appreciate the complementary value the two sayings offer? Values play a central role in human behavior. They shape norms and practices, define heroes, and establish symbols at the core of culture. Values influence not only attitudes and perceptions, but also choices.[35] As individuals get socialized from a young age, they internalize various values over their lifetime, including work values. According to Robert Roe and Peter Ester, "the importance of the role of work in many cultures makes work values into core

---

34. The theme of wealth creation is key in this reading. In other places in Proverbs (cf. 10:4; 16; 22; 14:24), the sages do not shy away from placing a positive value on wealth. The problem envisaged here may be the excessive desire for striving for wealth. Perhaps, the sage is drawing our attention to the one who pursues wealth. Although wealth's characterization as ephemeral puts a blip on its value, it is the pursuer who ultimately decides his/her actions relative to wealth. When wealth is pursued inordinately, it may create feelings of weariness and exhaustion. If this reading is taken, then the problem shifts to the one who pursues riches and the processes used to gain riches, and not the object of the pursuit.
35. Bardi and Schwartz, "Values and Behavior," 1208–10.

values that take a cardinal position in the overall pattern of values."[36] Definitions of work values focus on the goals individuals see as important and that they attempt to attain within their work context. Thus, work values are the desirable goals one pursues through labor.[37]

Scholars have identified three main types of work values: extrinsic, intrinsic, and social work values.[38] Extrinsic work values deal with the tangible outcomes from work such as pay, food, and job security. Intrinsic values deal with goals derived from the process of working such as job satisfaction. Intrinsic values differ from extrinsic work values; while the former is gained through the process of working, the latter is a result gained from the experience of the activity. Lastly, social work values deal with the relational benefits one gains within the work context such as friendship. Now, what work values do the two sayings offer as a basis for their respective messages?

Proverbs 14:23 uses extrinsic work values to promote hard work. This is discerned from the words "profit" (מוֹתָר) and "poverty" (מַחְסוֹר). The word מוֹתָר is a derivate of יָתַר ("a portion or a remaining part"). By associating hard work with מוֹתָר, the sage entices the audience with material possessions. As Waltke points out, the sense of excess is fundamental in the root יָתַר. Inversely, מַחְסוֹר devalues an individual.[39] Derived from the root חָסַר, מַחְסוֹר connotes meanings of lack and poverty.[40] The one who engages in unproductive conversations ends up poor, lacking even the basic necessities in life.

The word מוֹתָר, however, also carries the meanings of "advantage" and "pre-eminence."[41] Through hard work, one could

---

36. Roe and Ester, "Values and Work," 5.
37. Elizur, "Facets of Work Values," 379–89.
38. Elizur, "Facets of Work Values," 379–89; Kaasa, "Work Values in European Countries," 852–62; Ros et al., "Basic Individual Values," 49–71.
39. Waltke, *The Book of Proverbs*, 601.
40. Baker and Carpenter, *The Complete Word Study Dictionary*, 597.
41. Baker and Carpenter, *The Complete Word Study Dictionary*, 589.

attain several advantages, including gaining respect in the eyes of others. Being able to produce abundance through work is a sign of a responsible person with a preeminent character. Such a person, especially in a communal society like ancient Israel, is well-positioned to maximize life. From these meanings, מוֹתָר seems to project more than extrinsic motivation. In its abstract usage, מוֹתָר in the context of 14:23 projects nuanced motivations that could be intrinsic or social. For instance, the nuanced meaning of "advantage" is applicable in many contexts. Whereas the advantage here could certainly be the benefits one derives from producing in excess (extrinsic values). There is also the possibility that the meaning here is intangible, such as the advantage of experience one derives through working (intrinsic value) or the influence one could have over the others in the work context (social value).

Like 14:23, 23:4–5 may project more than one work value. Two verbs control the message of 23:4–5: תִּיגַע, "to be weary," and לְהַעֲשִׁיר, "to be rich." It is the latter, however, that the sage is concerned with. After the appearance of לְהַעֲשִׁיר in the first colon of v. 4, the remainder of the text develops this motif. The message is that wealth or riches can be ephemeral. The admonition against תִּיגַע is only in relation to the pursuit of the explicit goal of creating wealth. Wealth emerges as an extrinsic value in 23:4–5, although there is some level of reservation about it.[42] What is the sage's problem with the pursuit of wealth? Wealth can be deceptive. It can create frustration and disillusionment, one should be careful to not be fixated on wealth. If wealth is created through one's work, it is a good thing. However, one should not allow oneself to be controlled by the search for wealth in a way that causes exhaustion to the body.

It follows that the sage's reservation in 23:4–5 is about excessive desire and overly striving for wealth. In this case, the

---

42. Wealth is valuable in Proverbs. As Whybray, *Wealth and Poverty in the Book of Proverbs*, 113, indicates, Israelite sages with their Near Eastern counterparts shared the common view that wealth is a sign of blessing "though some qualify this assessment in various ways."

problem is not so much about wealth as it is the pursuer. Although it is wealth that receives negative evaluation, it is the pursuer who is advised to apply wisdom with respect to the pursuit of wealth. One does not become rich arbitrarily. As implied by the sage, the character of the one who becomes rich, as well as the manner in which wealth is attained are important.

While 14:23 exhorts and inspires audiences to believe in life's principle that hard work leads to gain, 23:4–5 adds the message that there is a need for caution when one's goal for working is to amass wealth; wealth can lead to exhaustion of body and can create frustration. Work should in no way compromise the life of the worker, no matter the goal for working. Intrinsic work values are implied in the wisdom offered here. Although hard work is good (as in 14:23) it should be carried out in a manner that optimizes life (23:4–5). Thus, even wealth (one of the most attractive goals for work) should not diminish the truth that work is for humans and not the reverse. The prohibition against hard work in 23:4, therefore, is in relation to the inordinate pursuit of wealth, a dangerous disposition to life. It can be argued that the two sayings complement each other in guiding their audiences into appreciating the complex relationship between work and its outcomes, especially wealth.

Proverbs 14:23 and 23:4–5, and their respective work values, point to the important role work plays in the socio-economic life of ancient Israelites. The prominence of extrinsic work values in the two texts shows ancient Israel's commitment to ensuring the sustenance of the society. In several sayings, work is promoted as the primary source of food, as well as income for basic needs (cf. 12:11; 19:15; 20:4; 27:23–26). Again, extrinsic work values reveal some aspect of ancient Israel's understanding of wealth creation. That is, hard work is encouraged as a socially acceptable way to create wealth (10:4; 12:11, 27; 13:4; 28:19), although in some cases (as in 23:4–5) the sages call for prudence when wealth becomes the main goal for work. The implied presence of intrinsic work values and social work values in the two sayings indicate the indispensable place of work in human life and the importance of social relations in the work context respectively. The centrality of work in the life of humans, for Israelite sages, is not only because through work individuals and societies achieve sustenance, but also that work is an integral part of what it means to be human. This idea is prominent in the characterization of the sluggard, who, because of the absence of work in his life, is depicted as a disillusioned figure (cf. 19:4; 22:13). Also, through work, individuals and society stand to benefit from the social bond that the work context provides. For instance, in 10:5, work presents the "son" (בֵּן) an opportunity to honor his family.

Conclusion

Proverbial sayings within these collections present many challenges. The absence of a performance context strips them of their dynamic social environs and in effect constrains their semantic range. As part of the wisdom tradition, however, Proverbs retains its associations with other wisdom books. Considered as the foundation of Israelite wisdom, conservative and optimistic, Proverbs is often contrasted with Job and Ecclesiastes where optimism dissipates and is replaced with doubts and skepticism. But as some scholars note, the suspicion against conservative wisdom has traces in Proverbs.[43] In the particular case of Prov 14:23 and 23:4–5, there appears to be a notable similarity in viewpoint and language with Ecclesiastes concerning ideas about labor and its place in human life. How can the Preacher's ideas help deal with the difficulties in comprehending the apparent contradictions of Prov 14:23 and 23:4–5?

In Prov 14:23, the sage exhorts the audience to have faith in hard work because it pays to work and to work hard. There is a gain to be accrued by the one who works hard. This idea coheres with the Preacher's message in Eccl 10:18 when he counsels against a slothful life. The optimism in these claims encourages the audience to make the choice for diligence instead of slothfulness. When this wisdom from 14:23 encounters that of 23:4–5, where on the surface reading the audience is advised to desist from hard work that wearies the body in order to create wealth,

---

43. See Crenshaw, *Old Testament Wisdom*, 229–50 and Dell, *The Book of Proverbs*, 83.

one may question the veracity of the claim in 14:23 or the utility of the counsel in 23:4–5. However, the two sayings offer valuable counsel on existential questions such as why we work, what outcomes we expect from our work, and the place of work in our total wellbeing.

Proverbs 14:23 lays the foundation for the inherent connection between humanity and work. The two are inseparable as long as humans continue to live. The phrase "in all labor" shows that the sage is not leaving out any form of work. In other words, one should not be concerned with the kind of work one engages in: so long as it is a legitimate work, one will not lose out. There is a benefit to work, be it extrinsic, intrinsic, or social, work is beneficial to individuals and society. The sage of the saying also directs readers to be conscious of why they engage in work. Working, which involves the exertion of energy, should not be done in vain. This message is important especially when many people consider their work worthless when they fail to gain material benefits from it. As explained above, the "advantage or gain" (מוֹתָר) of work can be realized in different forms.

This generic message of 14:23 is given a twist in 23:4–5, where this time the sage moves away from justifying the need for humans to work to illustrating the place of work in advancing the wellbeing of humans. By isolating the specific extrinsic value of wealth, the sage first affirms that hard work is one means through which wealth can be created. Indeed, in Eccl 10:19 the Preacher claims that money answers for everything (a claim which can be read cynically); however, the message may be that money does help in life. Wealth enhances human life in varied ways. But this is where the danger lies. Thus, through the rhetoric of 23:4–5, the sage places human life above wealth. Similarly, the Preacher notices that excessive wealth from one's toil can be problematic; not only does wealth dwindle, but also leads to sleepless nights. For the sage, the pursuit of wealth through hard work cannot rule one's life. If one allows the quest for wealth to overtake the good sense of optimizing how one works, then such a person is a fool. He misses out on the wisdom behind work and its value in human life.

As the Preacher implies in his message, labor is part of human fate. On the one hand, it helps one acquire pleasures for enjoyment, but on the other hand, it is a painful and frustrating experience (2:22–23) in which one is not guaranteed the enjoyment of one's profits as they may go to a fool (2:18), or another person (2:21). The message about labor, and its corollary, wealth, is not straight forward; it is a mystery the Preacher tries to fathom. Similarly, Prov 14:23 and 23:4–5 capture the intriguing relationship between human fate and human desire as it pertains to work and its role in human life. The wisdom here, perhaps, is that humans need to continuously rethink the place of work in our lives, and more importantly, the value placed on the benefits derived from work.

Bibliography

Baker, Warren, and Eugene Carpenter. *The Complete Word Study Dictionary: Old Testament*. Chattanooga, TN: AMG, 2003.

Bardi, Anat, and Shalom. H. Schwartz. "Values and Behavior: Strength and Structure of Relations." *Personality and Social Psychology Bulletin* 29 (2003) 1208–10.

Borowski, Oded. *Daily Life in Biblical Times*. Atlanta: Society of Biblical Literature, 2003.

Camp, Claudia. "Proverbs and the Problems of the Moral Self." *JSOT* 40 (2015) 25–42.

Clarke, Patrick. "Wisdom Literature and the Question of Priority —Solomon's Proverbs or Amenemope's Instruction." *Journal of Creation* 26 (2012) 50–56.

Collins, John J. *Introduction to the Hebrew Bible*. Englewood Cliffs, NJ: Prentice Hall, 1998.

Crenshaw, James L. *Old Testament Wisdom: An Introduction.* Louisville: Westminster John Knox, 2010.

Dell, Katharine J. *The Book of Proverbs in Social and Theological Context.* Cambridge: Cambridge University Press, 2006.

Elizur, D. "Facets of Work Values: A Structural Analysis of Work Outcomes." *Applied Psychology: An International Review* 69 (1984) 379–89.

Fox, Michael V. "The Formation of Proverbs 22:17—23:11." *Die Welt des Orients* 38 (2008) 22–37.

———. *Proverbs 1–9: A New Translation with Introduction and Commentary.* AB 18A. New Haven: Yale University Press, 2008.

———. *Proverbs 10–31: A New Translation with Introduction and Commentary.* AB 18B. New Haven: Yale University Press, 2009.

Hatton, Peter T. H. *Contradictions in the Book of Proverbs: The Deep Waters of Counsel.* Society for Old Testament Studies Monograph Series. Burlington, VT: Ashgate, 2008.

Kaasa, Anneli. "Work Values in European Countries: Empirical Evidence and Explanations." *Review of International Comparative Management* 12 (2011) 852–62.

Kitchen, K. A. "Basic Literary Forms and Formulations of Ancient Instructional Writings in Egypt and Western Asia." In *Studeien Zu Altägyptischen Lebenslehren*, edited by Erik Hornung and Othmar Keel, 235–92. Freiburg: Universitätsverlag Freiburg Schweiz, 1979.

———. "Proverbs and Wisdom Books of the Ancient Near East: The Factual History of a Literary Form." *TynBul* 28 (1977) 69–114.

Mieder, Wolfgang. *Proverbs: A Handbook.* Westport, CT: Greenwood, 2004.

Roe, Robert A., and Peter Ester. "Values and Work: Empirical Findings and Theoretical Perspectives." *Applied Psychology: An International Review* 48 (1999) 1–22.

Ros, M., et al. "Basic Individual Values, Work Values, and the Meaning of Work." *Applied Psychology* 48 (1999) 49–71.

Ruffle, John. "The Teaching of Amenemope and Its Connection with the Book of Proverbs." *Tyndale Bulletin* 28 (1977) 29–68.

Schwáb, Z. "The Sayings Clusters in Proverbs: Towards an Associative Reading Strategy." *JSOT* 38 (2013) 59–79.

Swanson, James A. *Dictionary of Biblical Language with Semantic Domains: Hebrew (Old Testament).* Oak Harbor, WA: Logos Research Systems, 1997.

Toy, C. H. *A Critical and Exegetical Commentary on the Book of Proverbs.* New York: C. Scribner's Sons, 1899.

Van Leeuwen, R. C. "Wealth and Poverty: Systems and Contradictions in Proverbs." *Hebrew Studies* 33 (1992) 25–36.

Waltke, Bruce K. *The Book of Proverbs: Chapters 1–15.* Grand Rapids: Eerdmans, 2004.

Westermann, Claus. *Genesis 1–11.* Translated by John J. Scullion. London: SPCK, 1984.

Whybray, R. N. *Wealth and Poverty in the Book of Proverbs.* LHBOTS 99. Sheffield: Sheffield Academic, 1990.

Yankah, Kwesi. "Do Proverbs Contradict?" *Folklore Forum* 17 (1984) 2–9.

Yodder, C. R. "Forming 'Fearers of Yahweh': Repetition and Contradiction as Pedagogy in Proverbs." *SWA* (2005) 167–84.

BEYOND BELIEF

Angeline Schellenberg[1]
Winnipeg, MB, Canada

A word—and water breathes,
trees surge with swallows.
Look, there in your fist:
a single globe atop
the barest stem, and tomorrow
dozens of dandelions startle
from cracks beyond the fence.

You are no different.
All it takes for oil to flow
is one empty flask.
Eve, when she held out
her thorny hand,
felt blossoms open.

---

1. Angeline Schellenberg is the author of two poetry collections. Her first book, *Tell Them It Was Mozart* (Brick Books, 2016), won the Lansdowne Prize for Poetry, the Eileen McTavish Sykes Award for Best First Book, and the John Hirsch Award for Most Promising Manitoba Writer. Her new book is *Fields of Light and Stone* (University of Alberta Press, 2020).

DO YOU THINK HUMANS WILL EVER WALK ON THE SUN?
—YAHOO INQUIRER[2]

Angeline Schellenberg
Winnipeg, MB, Canada

Some night when solar storms
throw off their feathers

we'll ascend through waxen clouds
and all their serenades.

Hang on a little longer, my dear.
This season may be dark but it's only

the sort of darkness
you'd find under the shadow

of a wing.

---

2. Inspired in part by the painting "The Heavens Declare . . . The Skies Proclaim" by Angela Lillico (www.angelalillico.com), which appears on the back cover of this issue of *MJTM*.

BEYOND LITERALISM AND LIBERALISM: UNDERSTANDING THE
GRAMMAR OF GENDERED LANGUAGE ABOUT GOD

Spencer M. Boersma
Acadia Divinity College, Wolfville, NS, Canada

A typical fault line in the debates between liberals and conservatives is the question of whether God can be referred to as "Mother." However, as this essay will endeavor to demonstrate, the binary of conservative versus liberal, and their accompanying methodological rules of either an appeal to revelation or appeal to experiential liberation, is problematic and in many ways a false dichotomy. Words must be understood by the contours of grammar that render them intelligible, where reference and function have intertwined capacities to offer meaning. In looking at several approaches (or "rules of grammar") of Christian thinkers who have commented on the structure of Christian discourse about God (following rules such as all discourse about God must be apophatic, analogical, narrative-driven, incarnation, trinitarian, etc.), a constructive convergence arises that challenges problematic understandings of both revelation and liberation.

Both approaches require a deeper "grammar." The philosopher Ludwig Wittgenstein noted that propositional statements find their fuller meanings in their forms of life.[1] Whether the same word refers to one thing or another is determined by the context of usage. In this regard, usage is often neglected in theological statements. When someone believes "in Jesus," which is undoubtedly the proper name of the second member of the Trinity, there has to be some reference to what that means in the speaker's actions in order to access the validity of their beliefs about "Jesus" and whether this is indeed the "Jesus" of the Christian Gospels. Surely, what a Mormon and a Roman

1. Wittgenstein, *Philosophical Investigations*, 111–12, 373.

Catholic mean when they affirm that they believe "in Jesus" is quite different even though they use to the same name. George Lindbeck pointed out that for a crusader who cried out "Christ is Lord" before killing innocent Muslims, "Christ" has a highly problematic meaning, as indicated by the form of life.[2] If Christian faith is like a language, where the context of usage is governed by the rules of grammar (such as when to use "a" or "an"), then Christian language is similarly intelligible because of the implicit grammars that structure it. What that structure is, implicit in speech, can be determined explicitly in order to hone communication. Thus, for theology to observe grammar as this essay will be doing, means several things for usage. When one examines some of the central ways Christians have structured discourse about God, one can see the means by which the two sides in this debate display perhaps not a resolution but at the least a strong convergence. In this regard, the concern for revelational realism (that is, that God reveals God's very self in word and historical events, especially in the life of Jesus Christ) and the concern for pragmatic liberation are not at loggerheads, but rather are complementary and go hand in hand.

So, what exactly is a name, grammatically speaking? There is no straightforward answer. While there are "proper names" like "Jesus" or "Yahweh," there are other categories of words that name God in a secondary sense: general words "God" or "El," titles like "El Shaddai" or "Christ," qualities such as "being" or "goodness," and still others that do not fit neatly into any category like Jesus being called "Immanuel." Are names arbitrary (or merely aesthetic as in today's culture) or are they irreducibly particular (and thus unreplaceable)? Or are names in the biblical narrative indicative of a certain denotation?[3] It seems that biblical names carried an important denotative function. Even a proper name like "Jesus" (which is of course not culturally accurate as it is actually "Yeshua") carried the connotation of being a Joshua-like savior figure for Israel. What this essay demonstrates is that there are multiple pathways through which God is named,

2. Lindbeck, *Nature of Doctrine*, 64.
3. Grenz, *The Named God*, 271–80.

though they do not replace the proper names Yahweh and Jesus, which aid in understanding masculine and father language as well as permit feminine and mother language. These pathways are holistically understood through the various grammars that offer deeper meaning to the divine identity.

The Current Debate: The Dichotomy Between the Rules of Revelation and Liberation

The two sides, which will be dubbed "conservative" and "feminist" for the purposes of this essay,[4] reveal a polarization in their considerations of how and why Christians can speak of God. In this regard, conservatives tend to assert the rule of Scripture while feminists assert the rule of liberating action.

Conservatives have typically asserted that God is "Father" and use the pronoun "he" because this is the language of Scripture. God in the Old Testament is most often referred to as "he" and Jesus, who is male and seen as a normative example, uses "Father" in addressing the first member of the Trinity. Thus, "Father" is the name of the first member of the Trinity and not merely a title or one metaphor among others. This argument, quite simple in form, is utilized by dozens of scholars.[5] In which, the baptismal language of the "name" of the "Father, Son, and Holy Spirit" (Matt 28:19), is essential to the identification of God. To attempt to supplant the baptismal formula or pray the

---

4. There is some reluctance in using these labels, as it will be shown that those that advocate usage of "Mother" can lay claim to the classical tradition of Christianity, and, on the other hand, can be committed to the classical tenants of Christianity which do not exclude and oppress women. It should be admitted that often feminist theologians then have been labelled "feminist" for pointing out the failure of many to see this, and these thinkers are then labelled "feminist theologians" where their critics are just "theologians." Thus, this essay from its opening terms is aware of how language and labels can function to marginalize some in a debate through the control of terms. No marginalization or dismissal is intended with either usage here.

5. Some examples are as follows: Packer, *Knowing God*, 183; Geffe, "'Father' as the Proper Name of God," 44; Bloesch, *Battle for the Trinity*; Pannenberg, *Systematic Theology*, 1:259–64; Kimel, *Speaking the Christian God*; Cooper, *Our Father in Heaven*; Biggs, "Gender and God-Talk," 15–25.

"Our Mother" instead of the "Our Father" (Matt 6:9–13; Luke 11:2–4) is tantamount to undermining what God has revealed. However, there is a diversity of perspectives within this view. Most would not argue that God is indeed truly male, but rather gendered pronouns are preferable to the depersonalized "it." Most would understand God as Father by revelation, but of course, would note that God is no created thing and is not male in a literal sense, reduced to a creature. Again, the implicit rule of this position might be stated as the language of the Bible legitimates the language that is permissible. Therefore, since Jesus did not refer to the first member of the Trinity as "Mother," the Church today is not allowed to say this either.[6] According to this grammar, God is named by revelation.

There are, of course, practical implications bound up with this view. This discussion can be tied to women in leadership. Particularly in Catholic theology, a female priest cannot represent Christ (who is male) the way a male is able to do.[7] Or in some conservative Protestant theology, a woman cannot lead (whether in a church, home, or society—there is a spectrum of what is allowable), because this forsakes a headship God has installed. Male headship coincides with divine headship.[8] There are plenty, however, who are convinced egalitarians, who do not see father language bound up with restricting women in leadership.[9]

Yet, many feminists worry that the use of male imagery alienates women and makes patriarchy more entrenched. Mary Daly famously said that if "God is male, then the male is god."[10]

---

6. Some essays that state that God is beyond gender, but that God cannot be referred to as Mother, seem to display a characteristic failure of integration of the biblical grammar. For an example see McGregor-Wright, "God, Metaphor, and Gender," 287–301. All the elements are present to affirm God as Mother, but the essay stops short. For many egalitarians in more conservative denominations or theological settings, resting at this position is a kind of theological safe place to say, "I am for equality of women, sure, but I am not liberal like those that insist God is Mother."
7. See "Declaration *Inter Insigniores*," 5.
8. See Grudem and Piper, eds., *Recovering Biblical Manhood and Womanhood*.
9. A good example is Bloesch, *Is the Bible Sexist*.
10. Daly, *Beyond God the Father*, 18.

Accordingly, male imagery is bound up with patriarchy and promotes the idea that God is closer to men. Thus, men are much more comfortable asserting authority over women and delegitimizing female experience in various forms, whether subtlety or in overtly abusive ways. Therefore, that which oppresses, namely women, must be negated and supplanted. This axiom has led to revisions to traditional language about God in order to prioritize feminine language as a counter against patriarchal language (as well as hierarchical images like "king" negated for ones like "friend").[11] Such a move is possible by an appeal to all language about God being metaphorical, as God is radically transcendent. Thus, for McFague, all images have their place, but certain ones like "king" or "father," that have held a dominant hegemony in Christianity, should be de-prioritized in the current climate to achieve pragmatic ends, namely that of liberation. One can see in this position a metaphorical approach that uses pragmatic concerns of liberation as its rule for how to speak of God: "The truth of theological formulation lies in its effects."[12]

Extremes on either side are apparent. The primary conservative weakness is that its strict appeal to the Bible results in literalism, which often seeks to uphold the "letter" so tightly it ironically misses the "spirit." The best aspect of this position asserts that the Bible prioritizes "he" and "Father" because this is the content of revelation. The notion that God reveals God's self is certainly fundamental to Christian faith. However, characteristic of literalism, there is often an emphasis on one detail that neglects others. A young earth creationist will insist that Gen 1 is a concrete, realistic narrative but has to ignore details in the text that describe a flat, domed universe. Similarly, literalization of God as father often downplays or ignores how God uses motherly language along with fatherly language in the Old Testament, which will be shown shortly. Literalism, ironically, misses a lot of what the Bible says and how it says it. A deeper analysis of the contents and grammar of scriptural speaking is needed.

11. McFague, *Models of God*, 165.
12. Carr, *Transforming Grace*, 109.

On the other side, there is a persistent tendency to downplay the authority of the Bible and realistic accounts of revelation. The notion that Scripture is rife with male language for God warrants, in this estimate, a sort of correcting or bypassing of it, seeing the Bible not as revelation or in any realistic sense as the Word of God.[13] Rosemary Radford Ruether states that her interpretive principle regards only those aspects of the biblical text that are useful to women's liberation to be authoritative, whereas the rest is to be "set aside and rejected."[14] Without a definite claim to revelation, however, metaphorical language has the potential to slip into projection of the human onto God, as Feuerbach accused theists of doing. Why one image is to be prioritized over another can potentially come down to one person's vision of liberation over another. The fact that someone like Jordan Peterson's highly hierarchical and male-dominant understandings of God are seen as appealing to many illustrates that liberation without realism of revelation can end up being perspectival and preferential and is at risk of devolving into Nietzschean self-assertion rather than the more counter-intuitive task of self-renunciation, compassion, and solidarity. This is, ironically, not practical. There are lots of forms of "liberal" theology today, some quite stimulating and self-consciously biblical. However, there are also unproductive forms that seek to undermine (or at the very least fail to uphold or bypass) a robust sense of the place of revelation and Scripture, imposing what seem to be concerns foreign to the biblical narrative upon it. In this regard, some approaches to God as "Mother" are this kind of liberalism.

While the primary concern of Christian feminism is to uphold the dignity of women as bearers of God's image, and in this regard, all Christians should be broadly feminist, there are expressions that are not concerned with being authentic to Christian faith or the kind of characteristic descriptions the Christian

---

13. See Schneiders, "The Bible and Feminism," 38–40. She argues for a "metaphorical" account of the Bible as the Word of God as central to feminist biblical interpretation in general.
14. Ruether, *Sexism and God-Talk*, 28.

community creates of itself and its narratives.[15] However, it should also be noted that some theological institutions and communities have made decisions that exclude women's voices or viable criticisms of the community's convictions. In this regard, some feminist criticism asserts that these exclusions are inherent to the structure of Christian discourse, and thus, in doing so, ironically concede their own marginalization as inherent to that discourse. Mary Daly notably left Christianity and deemed it inherently patriarchal.[16] This is not rhetorically effective, especially if it is not true. Thus, the following grammars, derived from the structures of the language of Scripture, will hopefully clarify the discourses of gendered language about God.

Ineffability and Negation

The first approach can be called "apophatic" (which means "negation"). The rule might be stated as follows: all discourse about God must recognize that God is transcendent and ineffable, and therefore, names and other language must be negated to prevent misconception.

Conservatives and feminists appeal to these schemes in two different ways. Conservatives use the apophatic approach to assert that God is beyond gender, but nevertheless, through realistic revelation God is exclusively male. The irony is that this language maintains that God is not gendered, while asserting that "he" cannot be anything other than the male gender. This is the impression of the Southern Baptist Convention's resolution in 1992: "God is beyond any human gender . . . [but] has uniquely and explicitly revealed himself to us as Father."[17] Meanwhile, some feminists have used ineffability to emphasize the radical transcendence of God above all language. The fusing of

---

15. This, admittedly, will look very different depending on the ecclesial community in question. This discussion will look very different in Canadian Baptist churches, where neither the literalism of biblical inerrancy nor motions against women in ministry have succeeded, as opposed to the Southern Baptist Convention.
16. Daly, *Beyond God the Father*, 140.
17. "Resolution on God the Father."

reference to this kind of exclusivity is viewed as idolatrous. However, some within this position seem to indicate that any revealed realism is also problematic, leaving language about God potentially agnostic.[18]

To clarify this rule, it was first and still perhaps best developed by the figure named Dionysius the Areopagite (named after the character from Acts 17:34, and often confused with his namesake). This writer from the late fifth to early sixth century was the first to devise a mystical approach of contemplating God. If God is truly ineffable and incomparable,[19] one implication of the disclosure of God's name to Moses, "I Am who I Am" (Exod 3:14), is that all language for God is in some way inadequate. God names God's self as unnameable.[20] Even the divine names for God must be negated to aid the believer in truly understanding how much higher God is than human thinking. Thus, Dionysius contemplates the words of Scripture, which he surely regards as revelation, and understands the deep grammar of this language. He sees God being named in transcendentals such as goodness, being, life, beauty, etc., which is important since God's names are not merely proper names. For each name, he is constantly aware of the fact that God is always so much more than any one biblical description. When God is described, an apophatic approach seeks to contemplate how God is also "not" that in order to respect God's ineffability. Some examples from his writings are instructive. For instance, he states that God is being. However, he argues that God is "not existent" or not "being," as God's being is simply beyond all existence as humans know it.[21] What is more interesting is that Dionysius will at times use opposing language to aid in negation. Unlike the later metaphysical tradition, he holds that God is both "being" and "becoming," "eternal" and "momentary," "past" and "future."[22]

    18.   McFague, *Models of God*, 35. She also notably writes that religious language applies "only to our existence, not God's" (39).
    19.   One should note that this is also the starting point for some feminists. See Johnson, *She Who Is*, 105.
    20.   Dionysius, *On the Divine Names*, 1:1.
    21.   Dionysius, *On the Divine Names*, 1:1.
    22.   Dionysius, *On the Divine Names*, 5:3.

In doing so, he seeks to demonstrate that God is also beyond all of these. God's light is so beyond, it appears as "darkness";[23] God's word speaks as silence, etc. God is even conceived to be beyond every negation as well. The names of the Trinity are "titles" for Dionysius. They are irreducible in that they point to the unity within the diversity of the activities of the ineffable God.[24] Sadly, Dionysius's treatment on divine symbols for God is lost (one of the great tragedies of theological history), and the mentions of other conceptual names of God neglect awareness of feminine imagery.[25] However, to extrapolate, one could argue that it is fully consistent with Dionysius's approach to uphold both that God is Father, and beyond fatherliness, and to negate this, he might use, "Mother" (not that male-female is equivalent to the other binaries discussed).

Therefore, if God is ineffable, it is important to establish that language for God should be negated and it can often be negated with opposite language. Dionysius does not deny realistic revelation, but rather sees its deeper grammar in which any name for God must be negated. Thus, one of the earliest ways of structuring Christian discourse reveals a deep congruence with both ways of referring to God.

Analogy and Metaphor

The second classic way Christian language has been organized is the way of analogy (comparisons using "like" or "as" to communicate meaning based on a corresponding partial similarity) and metaphor (the creative application of similarity of two dissimilar things to communicate an abstract quality that the other has concretely).[26] God is the being of all beings, all that which is good

23. Dionysius, *Mystical Theology*, 1:1.
24. Dionysius, *On the Divine Names*, 2:3.
25. Dionysius, *On the Divine Names*, 1:6; 1:8.
26. This essay uses basic definitions of metaphor, but for more in-depth treatments, see Soskice, *Metaphor and Religious Language*, as well as Ricoeur, *The Rule of Metaphor*.

in existence can be used analogically to describe what God is like, and in so far as God is dissimilar from existence, creation can still nevertheless be employed to describe God's qualities metaphorically.

Analogy and metaphor are employed differently by conservatives and feminists. Conservatives, such as Colin Gunton, grant metaphorical language and analogy, but do so from a basis of underlying realism concerning historical revelation.[27] When it relates to the divine name, it is, nevertheless, not metaphorical. The possibility of referring to God as Mother, even metaphorically, or having feminine qualities and body parts, has been routinely critiqued as edging on paganism, polytheism, and pantheism. For instance, Elizabeth Achtemeier argues that feminine language cannot be used because it is prone to paganism, undermining God's transcendence.[28] Wolfhart Pannenberg argues that sexual differentiation in God would mean polytheism.[29] Meanwhile, feminists, such as Sallie McFague, argue that religious language is entirely metaphorical,[30] emphasizing that even the divine name is metaphorical to the point that it is a human construction that humans can preferentially change.[31] Thus, expositing the language of Scripture according to this rule will add clarity in how metaphors can be realistic and offer liberty of usage without being imposed constructs.

These rules were supremely developed by Thomas Aquinas. Aquinas himself was deeply indebted to Dionysius (assuming him incorrectly to be the writer from Acts). Similarly, Aquinas held that God was ineffable, but also noted that if God is the "I Am," then God is perfect being, "the One Who Is."[32] God's being is what holds all being together. God's goodness is the

---

27. Gunton, "Proteus and Procrustes," 65–80. Gunton offers in many ways an agreeable critique to McFague, but goes too far in insisting that everyone who seeks to permit mother language denies realistic revelation the way she does.
28. Achtemeier, "Exchanging God for 'No Gods,'" 8.
29. Pannenberg, *Systematic Theology*, 1:261.
30. McFague, *Metaphorical Theology*, 99, 134.
31. McFague, *Metaphorical Theology*, 15–16.
32. Aquinas, *Summa Contra Gentiles*, 1:22:10.

goodness of all beings, who are essentially good as created things despite displaying characteristic privations of goodness from the fall. This means that any goodness in nature is analogous to God's goodness.[33] If something is, for instance, beautiful, it is such because this beauty is in some way like God's beauty as it participates and finds its being in God. Yet, since God is beyond all beings, the analogical way incorporates Dionysius's negative way: God is like the goodness of created beings, but not equated with them.[34]

This analogical axiom is made explicit in passages like Isa 66:13a, "As a mother comforts her child, I will comfort you."[35] Additionally, if God is exclusively like a "he" or "father" and simply can never be like a "she" or "mother," this would seem to indicate a domain where God is absent, which does not seem to be in keeping with how both male and female are in the divine "image" (Gen 1:26–27).[36] One is given the distinct impression that fatherliness as a quality participates in God's being and goodness in a higher degree than motherliness.

Aquinas grants a link between analogy and metaphor.[37] Scripture affirms that God is metaphorically a rock, lion, wind, fire, etc. God is strong and dependable like a rock, regal and untamed like a lion, invisible like wind, etc. God takes on metaphorical titles like king, shepherd, warrior, etc. and these communicate their own positive qualities. All of these metaphors are

33. Aquinas, *Summa Contra Gentiles*, 1:34:1.
34. Aquinas, *Summa Contra Gentiles*, 1:14:2.
35. This is a part of a peculiar passage (Isa 66:10–13) where Jerusalem is personified as a woman nursing Israel, whom God has restored, but then God embodies this analogy such that God seems to participate in the references to "her."
36. McFague, *Models of God*, 98. Also see Jewett, *God, Creation, and Revelation*, 323–25.
37. Aquinas, *Summa Contra Gentiles*, 1:30:2: "Since it is possible to find in God every perfection of creatures, but in another and more eminent way, whatever names unqualifiedly designate a perfection without effect are predicated of God and of other things: for example, goodness, wisdom, being, and the like. But when any name expresses such perfections along with a mode that is proper to a creature, it can be said of God only according to likeness and metaphor."

appropriate as their concrete goodness as created things point in different ways to how God is uniquely good.[38] This fittingness even makes possible motherly metaphors from the animal kingdom: whether it is a bird or eagle caring for its young (Ps 91:4) or a mother bear communicating God's fierceness in judgment (Hos 13:8).[39]

Metaphorical description is the grammar that stands behind many passages that employ motherly and feminine language. God describes God's self to Moses metaphorically as the mother and nurse of Israel, birthing and nursing Israel: "Did I conceive all this people? Did I give birth to them, that you should say to me, 'Carry them in your bosom, as a nurse carries a sucking child, to the land that you promised on oath to their ancestors?'" (Num 11:12). Similarly, titles of God like *El Shaddai*, God Almighty, where *shaddai* may be derivative from *shadu,* meaning "breasts," suggests God's power over creation is like human fertility.[40] Also, Deuteronomy uses motherly and rock metaphors to warn, "You have forgotten the rock who bore you and put out of mind the God who gave you birth" (Deut 32:18). Job 38:8–9, 28–29, Jer 31:20, and Isa 46:3–4 all describe God as having borne Israel. This language is taken up in the description of the Trinity in the eleventh council of Toledo in 675 CE, which describes the Son as begotten from the "womb of the father." Aquinas does not draw from this implication when he discusses

---

38. Aquinas (*Summa Contra Gentiles*, 1:31:2) gives an example in the next section after discussing metaphor where a stone is not a proper name of God the way wisdom is (although he oddly neglects the scriptures that do refer to God as a rock here), nevertheless, a stone "imitates God as its cause in being and goodness."

39. There are other uses of feminine language that employs cultural language that refers to typically female roles. God is portrayed as a midwife attending a birth in Pss 22:9–10, 71:6, and Isa 66:8–9. Paralleling God as shepherd (male) in the parables, God and his kingdom are described as being like a woman working leaven into bread (Luke 13:21) and a woman seeking a lost coin (Luke 15:8–10), both chores of Galilean peasant women. Jesus identifies God in these parables with women.

40. See Gen 17:1; 28:3; 35:11; 43:14; 48:3; 49:25. Several of these coincide with themes of fertility, thus corroborating the connotation. See Biale, "The God with Breasts," 240–56. Also see, Mollenkott, *The Divine Feminine.*

the Trinity, but other writers do. Clement of Alexandria writes concerning the Son, "The Word is everything to his little ones, both father and mother and tutor and nurse."[41] He goes on and speaks of the breasts of the Father, Son, and Spirit that nourish the church.[42] Similarly, John Chrystostom hails God as, "Thou art my Father, thou art my Mother, thou my Brother, thou art Friend, thou art Servant, thou art House-keeper; thou art the All, and the All is in thee; thou art Being, and there is nothing that is, except thou."[43]

These descriptions should show that the criticism of motherly and feminine language by conservative proponents cannot be maintained. The accusations of connection to paganism and polytheism are stunningly neglectful of the above passages, which make it abundantly clear that female anatomy and motherly descriptions do not by necessity imply this connection. The fact that they are criticized as such could be indicative of deep-seated unconscious prejudice, or in turn fuel it.

In the analogical and metaphorical grammar of referring to God, to deny motherly language to God is to deny both the created goodness of motherliness and the appropriate capacity for creaturely motherliness to render God's redemptive love, as Scripture and certain writers in the Christian tradition have shown. Whether or not "Mother" is a proper name for the first member of the Trinity is still to be discussed, but as a metaphorical and analogical means of referring to God, classic Christian discourse more than allows this, given the richness of images and titles used.

---

41. Clement of Alexandria, *Christ the Educator*, 68.
42. Clement of Alexandria describes God the Father at length as the Mother who nurses God's children: " . . . little ones who seek the Word, the craved for milk is given from the Father's breasts of love for man." *Christ the Educator*, 43. Similarly, Teresa of Avila, *Interior Castle*, 179–80, "For from those divine breasts where it seems God is always sustaining the soul there flows streams of milk bringing comfort to all people." See also Haddad, "Feminine God Language."
43. Chrysostom, *Homilies on the Gospel of Saint Matthew*, 447.

Narrative

The third approach is a narrative approach. This rule would state that God is described through the events in Israel's history that offer definition to God's essential character.

Again, there is a strange dichotomy here. For conservatives, there is a strong appeal to realistic revelation. There is often a neglect, as previously shown, of feminine imagery in favor of prioritizing the father language in narratives and understanding it as being about the gender of God's agency (or that the agency of God can only be communicated with one particular gender). Meanwhile, feminist often deny the historicity of revelation and even use the description "fiction"[44] with an affirmation of the existence of feminine imagery.

As Ricoeur argues, "The naming of God is thus first of all a narrative naming. The theology of tradition names God in accord with a historical drama that recounts itself as a narrative of liberation . . . It is these events that name God."[45] The analogical and metaphorical ways are susceptible to projection and confusion that make them dependent on being understood through God's acts in history as concrete descriptors for Israel's worship.[46] Here, the revelation of God as "I am who I am," cannot be forgotten. As Ricoeur writes, "the revelation of the name is the dissolution of all anthropomorphisms, of all figures and figurations, including that of the father. The name against the idol."[47] God is a rock, but God is not found in idols. God is a whirlwind, but when Jesus rebukes the storm, presumably he is not rebuking his own presence. Aquinas is more than aware of these kinds of confusions, and so, his own way of analogically understanding God moves from affirmation and negation to what he calls the way of eminence, in which a purer way of referring is possible.[48] An isolated metaphor for God must be understood within the

---

44. McFague, *Models of God*, xi, "theology is mostly fiction."
45. Ricoeur, "Naming God," 225.
46. See Wright, *God who Acts*.
47. Ricoeur, "Fatherhood," 486.
48. Aquinas, *Summa Contra Gentiles*, 1:30.4. See Long, *Speaking of God*, 149–215, for an account of these uses of language in Aquinas.

narrative patterns of God's actions. Coinciding with the preceding rule, what this shows is that the characteristic behavior of God is described with a diversity of descriptions and that these descriptions, whether fatherly or motherly, are not referring to God's gender but rather to God's goodness and love.

The title "Father" is given concrete description in the narratives of Israel. This is essential to how God communicates to ancient patriarchal culture that worshiped the "father of the gods" and whose families were ruled by a patriarch. Because God is powerful and because men were powerful in the ancient culture, one sees the analogical reference of God as Father. Feminists are correct to criticize this in that women did have a low worth in this culture which factors into this prioritization, but the biblical narrative shows a characteristic surmounting of patriarchy in and through this accommodation.[49] God was like these supreme gods in authority and God was like a father: creating, providing, protecting, promising, blessing, etc. However, this becomes a pathway of saying that when one looks at the narrative actions of God used to define God's self, God is much more than these. There is both a metaphorical employment and narrative subversion similar to Aquinas's affirmation and negation. God was not merely the central god of the ancient pantheon, but rather, called Abraham out of this belief, out of his father's household, and into a new reality of God's loving care, one then surmounts the regionalization of deity or the brutality of child sacrifice, etc. Similarly, God's fatherliness is central to God delivering his "firstborn" Israel out of Egypt (Exod 4:23). As this Father God is the God that made promises to the fathers of Israel, so also, God delivers his oppressed children, protecting them and giving them a new inheritance (Exod 6:6–8). Thus, the fatherly quality of God counters oppression and reiterates that God is unlike any other. There are moments then that surmount patriarchy as fatherly metaphors were used to speak of God's care in light of Israel's waywardness, and so, the coldness of an unloving

---

49. For a good analysis of how the Bible has been both repressive as well as the means of redemption, and how to understand these in interpretation, see Webb, *Slaves, Women, and Homosexuals*.

patriarch is transformed into a symbol of God's incomparable love: the father that never stops loving his children, unlike any other father. Isaiah invokes father language as a means of mercy: "Yet, O Lord, you are our father. We are the clay, you are the potter; we are all the work of your hand. Do not be angry beyond measure, O Lord; do not remember our sins forever" (Isa 64:7–9).[50] Similarly, Jeremiah sees God's fatherliness as incomparable love in the midst of Israel's rebellion: "They will come with weeping; they will pray as I bring them back. I will lead them beside streams of water on a level path where they will not stumble, because I am Israel's father, and Ephraim is my firstborn son" (Jer 31:9; cf. Jer 3:19). Hosea identifies God as a lover, whose wife cheated on him, but then the metaphor shifts seamlessly into father language and into a moment of tenderness:

> When Israel was a child, I loved him, and out of Egypt I called my son . . . It was I who taught Ephraim to walk, taking them by the arms; but they did not realize it was I who healed them. I led them with cords of human kindness, with ties of love. To them I was like one who lifts a little child to the cheek, and I bent down to feed them . . . How can I give you up, Ephraim? How can I hand you over, Israel? . . . My heart is changed within me; all my compassion is aroused. I will not carry out my fierce anger, nor will I devastate Ephraim again. For I am God, and not a man—the Holy One among you. I will not come against their cities (Hos 11:1, 3–4, 8–9).

But it cannot be neglected that while fatherly language is prioritized, in a time when there were many cold, unloving patriarchs, to indeed counter patriarchy, there is also an employment of motherly metaphors that is aware that this motherly language also does not fully grasp the narratives of God's faithful love.

---

50. It should be noted that the writer also uses the relation of father to lament and accuse God of hardening the hearts of Israel in a bizarre but powerfully relational moment in Scripture: "Where are your zeal and your might? Your tenderness and compassion are withheld from us. But you are our Father, though Abraham does not know us or Israel acknowledge us; you, O Lord, are our Father, our Redeemer from of old is your name. Why, O Lord, do you make us wander from your ways and harden our hearts, so we do not revere you? Return for the sake of your servants, the tribes that are your inheritance" (Isa 63:15–17).

Isaiah 49:15 says, "Can a mother forget the baby at her breast and have no compassion on the child she has borne? Though she may forget, I will not forget you!" (notice the apophatic approach implicitly at work in motherly language as well). God loves like a mother, but even then, is more loving than that. These descriptions also resist a simple bifurcation of fatherly qualities as power and wrath where motherly is tender and compassionate. Isaiah uses mother metaphors to communicate wrath, the wrath of a woman in labor:

> But now, like a woman in childbirth, I cry out, I gasp and pant . . . I will lay waste the mountains and hills and dry up all their vegetation . . . I will lead the blind by ways they have not known, along unfamiliar paths I will guide them; I will turn the darkness into light before them and make the rough places smooth. These are the things I will do; I will not forsake them (Isa 42:14–16).

Thus, to reiterate, it seems that both sets of language are employed, not to make a statement of God's gender but to richly describe the incomparable love God has for Israel.

Robert Hamerton-Kelly comments on this dynamic,

> Among the prophets, God is called father directly, in order to emphasize his care for his people, as a foil to their sin—sin as an expression of ingratitude. Throughout the prophetic stage, whether the symbolization is direct or indirect, explicit or implied, there is a tendency to move back and forth between 'father' and 'mother' imagery. The symbol described as that of a 'parent,' with a preponderance of the 'father' element . . . Fatherliness (and motherly language) becomes less about the social order of power and more about 'a symbol of free relationship and divine kindness.'[51]

The central confession of Israel was based on God's forgiveness after the idolatry of the golden calf where Moses beholds God's identity as "the Lord" and therefore as a "compassionate and gracious God, slow to anger, abounding in love and faithfulness" (Exod 34:6–7). As Brueggemann notes, this "credo of adjectives" runs through the whole Old Testament.[52] This suggests

---

51. Hamerton-Kelly, *God the Father*, 51.
52. See Brueggemann, *Old Testament Theology*, 213–28.

that fundamental to the divine essence is not gender, but agapeic love, the former employed to illustrate the latter. For this reason, Jürgen Moltmann suggests language such as "God our motherly Father and fatherly Mother."[53] Thus, the grammar of narrative adds further concrete description to gendered language, showing the legitimacy of analogical and metaphorical language but also revealing the incomparable love of God and coinciding with the apophatic, as revealed in the acts of God and events of history.

Incarnation

The fourth approach, which is perhaps a cluster of connected approaches, might be called Christocentric. Discourse about God must be in conformity with the incarnation, cross, and resurrection of Jesus Christ. It explores how revelation in Scripture finds its apex and center in Jesus Christ. Coinciding with the apophatic grammar, God is ineffable, yet can paradoxically be revealed in the finite. God reveals God's self in creation and history. Thus, the *Logos* of creation, through whom "all things were made" (John 1:3), reinforces the analogical way of referring. Coinciding with the narrative pattern, the male identity and language of Jesus is not a reification of God's gender so much as an illustration of God's love and thus actually serves to subvert patriarchy.

In conservative and feminist theologies, misappropriations and misunderstandings occur over the nature of Jesus. Some conservatives see the maleness of Jesus as insurmountable in these discussions. Thus Ray Anderson writes, "One can call God 'Mother' by switching metaphors but one cannot make Jesus into a female."[54] Some then have used this to overtly legitimate patriarchy by claiming that Jesus is male because maleness is required to have the authority to teach and govern.[55]

---

53. Moltmann, "The Fatherly Mother," 51–56.
54. Anderson, "The Incarnation of God," 288. One should note that Anderson does permit "mother" metaphors, as the above quotation shows, but these are of a different sort to the language of Jesus's maleness and therefore God's Fatherliness.
55. For a popular but truly reprehensible example, see Matthis, "Why Jesus Was Not A Woman."

In some feminist theology, there is an objection to Jesus's maleness as incapable of redeeming women. Ruether writes,

> Today a Christology which elevates Jesus's maleness to ontologically necessary significance suggests that Jesus's humanity does not represent women at all. Incarnation does not include women, therefore women cannot be redeemed. That is to say, if women cannot represent Christ, then Christ does not represent women.[56]

She continues on to say that the particularly of Jesus's humanity is problematic, "Jesus's maleness as essential to his ongoing representation not only is not compatible but is contradictory to the essence of his message as good news to the marginalized *qua* women."[57] Others seek to bypass classical Christology. Sallie McFague has stated, "I have not found it possible as a contemporary Christian to support an incarnational Christology or a canonical Scripture; nevertheless, I have found it possible to support a 'parabolic' Christology and Scripture as the Christian classic."[58] Scripture is not so much an authority so much as a beginning point and holding to Christ as merely a "parable" suggests an inability to incorporate historicity with Jesus's identity. Therefore, "Christ" is a linguistic and metaphorical phenomenon, not a historical, realistic one.[59] But if the historical particularity of Jesus is upheld, the question must be addressed on those terms: How can a male savior show God's presence to women? Why did Jesus not come as a woman or as non-gendered?

Here, the incarnational must be understood through the narrative of Jesus's life. The fact that his teaching elevated the dignity of women cannot be overlooked,[60] and thus, his reference to God

---

56. Ruether, "The Liberation of Christology," 140.
57. Ruether, "The Liberation of Christology," 147.
58. McFague, *Metaphorical Theology*, viii.
59. For a survey on approaches to the historical Jesus, see Powell, *Jesus as a Figure in History*. More nuanced approaches to the historical Jesus that describes that narrative as realistic revelation include Frei, *The Identity of Jesus Christ* and Johnson, *The Real Jesus*.
60. While this will not be pursued in detail here, it should be noted that there is quite a comfortable consensus between evangelical egalitarians, feminist, and liberal scholarship. Johnson, *Consider Jesus*, 108–10. Also see, Spencer, "Jesus's Treatment of Women," 126–41.

as "Abba" further reiterates the liberating and incomparable love the prophets preached. Moreover, his life culminates in the cross. The feminist theologian Elizabeth Johnson makes the case that the maleness of Jesus offers the "kenosis of patriarchy . . . for a man to live and die in this way in a world of male privilege is to challenge the patriarchal ideal of the dominating male at its root."[61] Something similar can be said of how Jesus is a "king." Jesus can be said to be king in the sense of his royal lineage going back to David, thus he was identifiable as the messiah. But does this merely uphold the authority of human kings? It has been used this way just as father language has been used to uphold patriarchy. But this is a misunderstanding. His particular way of being the messianic king is very different than the way other kings operate. Jesus is a king without wealth or military might or earthly splendor. Jesus's kingship is shown through his servanthood as he washed his disciples' feet, and supremely in his humiliation in becoming "last" on the cross (Mark 10:31–45). The narrative, both ironically and accurately, notes the sign above him at the cross which reads, "King of the Jews," as Jesus's reign is cruciform not oppressive. It is glorious because it is humble. Jesus's kingdom is the cross, self-sacrificial love with complete obedience to righteousness. Thus, if a king (or any leader) seeks to be a king like Jesus, to wield capability this way, they would be obliged to do so in a completely humble and even powerless way.[62] This is important to keep in mind as well because most conservatives are theologically in favor of democracy and not a strict monarchy, suggesting the kingship of Jesus can make possible the negation of human monarchy into a form of government that upholds the spirit of Jesus's kingdom.

Similarly, the maleness of Jesus should in fact be used to call into question patriarchy with Jesus's kenosis of power.

---

61. Johnson, *Consider Jesus*, 111. Similarly, LaCugna writes, "The total identification of God with Jesus the Son, even unto death on a cross, makes impossible to think of God as a distant, omnipotent monarch who rules the world just as any patriarch rules over his family and possessions." LaCugna, "Baptismal Formula," 243.

62. Similarly, to be a "citizen of heaven" (Phil 3:20) calls into question any nationalist view of citizenship.

Athanasius writes, "Men are not really fathers and really sons, but shadows of the True."[63] Similarly, Paul Ricoeur notes that it is in the Son, who is at one with the Father, that there is the decisive rejection of Freudian projections.[64] It must be maintained, then, that metaphorical reference begins a process of conceptualizing God's love, and God's actions in Jesus Christ fully particularize and define God through the narrative. Names and titles carry denotation, but they are only fully clarified through the full scope of a character's action.

As patriarchy is shown to be rooted in the curse of Eve, "your desire will be for your husband but he will rule over you" (Gen 3:16), and as a part of the death of sin entering the world, Jesus's resurrection shows the victory over this sin. The Father raises the Son, further implying this language is counter-oppressive in the possibilities of hope it opens. In the Pentecost formation of the church, the incarnation continues by incorporating people into Christ's body. While the church is not Jesus in one sense, this language does show the inclusion of all races, classes, and gender into Christ. Thus, while the historical Jesus is male (and Jewish), the exalted Jesus, by the Spirit, takes on all flesh into the body of Christ.[65] Thus, writers like Clement are in a sense correct to argue that Christ has both a male and a female nature. The incarnation (though he does not distinguish between pre- and post-resurrected identity) is the assumption of all human nature in Jesus in conformality with God's essence of love:

> For what further need has God of the mysteries of love? And then you shall look into the bosom of the Father, whom God the only-begotten Son alone has declared. And God Himself is love; and out of love to us became feminine. In His ineffable essence He is Father; in His compassion to us He became Mother. The Father by loving became feminine: and the great proof of this is He whom He begot of Himself; and the fruit brought forth by love is love.[66]

---

63. Athanasius, *Four Discourses*, ch. 6.
64. Ricoeur, "Fatherhood."
65. This is laid out in Johnson, "Redeeming the Name of Christ: Christology," 129.
66. Clement of Alexandria, "Who is the Rich Man?," 37.

Clement is one of many writers that sees Jesus's concern for Israel wanting to "gather her chicks under her wings" (Matt 23:37–38) as displaying a nature, while historically male, nevertheless, is fully reconciled with femininity. And thus, the title "Mother Christ" is attested to in several writers such as Anselm,[67] Bernard of Clairvaux,[68] and Julian of Norwich (who will be discussed later). Such pairing within the early Christian tradition demonstrates that while masculine language is conventional, it is not exclusive. In fact, when one understands what it is saying, the reason why Jesus's maleness works for all humanity is the very reason it permits femininity: it shows God's agapeic love.

If Jesus is God Immanuel, present to all creation and all flesh, who taught the lifting up of women, the self-emptying of patriarchy in the cross, and the defeat of sin in the resurrection, then the pattern of Jesus offers a way of understanding both male and female language. Could these contours of Christology render the possibility of a creative and disruptive depiction of Jesus as female? Certainly, similar licenses are taken with Jesus's ethnicity to reiterate the incarnation of Jesus of all flesh. Is the depiction of Jesus as "Christa," like the crucifix sculpted by Edwina Sandys (in 2016) that hangs in St. John the Divine Church in New York, actually theologically accurate?

Trinitarian

The fifth grammar that structures Christian discourse is trinitarian. How one speaks of God must conform to the structure where God reveals the oneness of God's being in three persons of eternal loving relationship and unified action. Paul described the three identities of God perhaps best in his benediction in 2 Cor

---

67. Anslem writes, "And you, Jesus, are you not also a mother? Are you not the mother who, like a hen, gathers her chickens under her wings?" Anselm, *The Prayers and Meditations*, 153.

68. Bernard of Clairvaux (*Letter 322*): "Do not let the roughness of our life frighten your tender years. If you feel the stings of temptation . . . suck not so much the wounds as the breasts of the Crucified. He will be your mother, and you will be his son" (quoted in Bynum, *Jesus as Mother*, 117).

13:14, "May the grace of the Lord Jesus Christ, and the love of God, and the fellowship of the Holy Spirit be with you all." The Trinity in John's writings displays a pattern of love in God's essence that the disciples are invited into (John 15:9–17; 17:20–23; 1 John 4:7–21).

Trinitarian grammar in conservative theology has been used to support the notion that the first member of the Trinity is definitively named "Father," committing a literalization of what this means. This is not without warrant in church history, as Tertullian refused it as an analogical title: "Whereas other analogical terms like Lord and Judge indicate a merely functional relation to the world, the names Father and Son point to an ontological relation of distinct persons within the godhead itself."[69] But is it necessarily the case that because father language is realistic it therefore creates an exclusive ontological reference?

Meanwhile, in feminist theology, McFague would not see the trinitarian language of Father, Son, and Spirit as "naming" God so much as offering a three-fold metaphor of God's mystery, physicality, and mediation.[70] This is reminiscent of a modalism that, as the early church thinkers warned, does not do justice to the three-fold personal revelation that upholds God's identity as love itself. If God's identity as love itself is lost, something vital to liberation is lost with it. Just as literalism ironically misses key features and intentions of the biblical text, the pragmatic approach can, by having a reaction against biblical authority and realistic revelation, undermine the means within the Christian community whereby liberation can be endorsed. Thus, the following clarifications are necessary.

First, "Father" is not the proper name of the first member of the Trinity. The maleness of Jesus, his message of the loving God as "Abba" (Mark 14:36; Rom 8:15; Gal 4:6—one should note also that then "Abba" is not employed in three out of four Gospels), his self-emptying in the cross, and vindication in

---

69. Tertullian, *Adversus Praxean*, 9–10, as quoted in Bloesch, *Word and Spirit*, 295n77.
70. McFague, *The Body of God*, 193.

resurrection all support father language as counter-patriarchal.[71] Does this mean father language is irreplicable? Is "Father" the definitive name of God, the first member of the Trinity? Some argued that the names of the Trinity replace Yahweh in the New Testament.[72] Those who advocate this forget that Jesus used a more intimate term: "Abba." Accordingly, "Father" is not the name of the first member of the Trinity just as "Son" is not Jesus's given name. God's primary name, as R. Kendall Soulen points out, is and remains, the ineffable "I Am." Father, Son, and Spirit, are, as he calls them, "inflections" that reveal relational roles that bear witness to how the oneness of the "I Am" has three personal identities.[73] What this means is that "father" is not a name per se so much as a term of endearment, witnessing to how Jesus bears the messianic title of "Son." These identities act as a coordinating witness in Jesus's baptism, ministry of proclaiming the kingdom, his transfiguration, and especially his death on the cross and resurrection. They are relational roles identifying the narrative character of God's ineffable love. Context is not all determining, but neither is it irrelevant. Jesus reiterates "Father" because of its capacity to communicate the incomparable love the prophets preached over and against the austerity and arrogance of the Pharisees' understanding of how they were children of "Father Jacob" and "Father Abraham" (John 4:12; 8:56). The fact that the Father and the Spirit are identified with male pronouns are not reifications of God's gender so much as witnesses of God's identification with Jesus Christ's work, whose own maleness as already been explained in the previous rule. For the Gospels, the title "Father" is showing not the gender of the first member of the Trinity, nor even a biological relation between Father and Son, but Jesus as the fulfillment of the character of the God of the Old Testament. While "Father" is used in the Gospels, as previously noted, the portraits of God in the Old Testament were not exclusively male. Thus, the

71. This is similarly argued in Visser't Hooft, *The Fatherhood of God*.
72. Particularly adamant is Kimel, "The God who Likes His Name," 188–208.
73. Soulen, "The Name of the Holy Trinity," 244–61.

vindication of God's identity in Jesus is shown through the "Father" but this action is not exclusively bound or understood exclusively through one word describing a male-gendered parent. This is a warranted abstraction. In classic theology, the title "Father" cannot be literalized, as Arius used the notion that God is the father of Jesus to imply that there was a time when the Son was not, as no son is the same age as his father. To this, the title "Father" and language of being "begotten" had to be abstracted and qualified to respect the divinity of the Son. Likewise, "Father" cannot be used to speak concretely of gender either, and if its use is not about gender, insisting on it can miss its very meaning. Insisting on it as a proper name as a denotative literalization then misses what it is trying to communicate, and risks supplanting the "I Am" name of God to which the triune identities point, along with the other biblical images, that give meaning to God's action.

This means that the baptismal phrase "in the name of the Father, Son, and Spirit" is not inherently offensive, but it does invite a deeper explanation to prevent misusage. As a way of witnessing to the character of the "I Am" God in Jesus Christ, it must not be understood apart from its essentially counter-patriarchal form, which it sadly often has. But does this mean that mother language cannot be substituted in? Traditionalists have tried to insist that it cannot, meanwhile revisionists have offered all sorts of alternatives, which often appear awkward or even modalist (such as McFague's suggestion). Nevertheless, "Mother, Son, and Spirit" is permissible alongside the classic language based on the analogical and metaphoric grammars previously stated, but one does so at the risk of giving the impression of misunderstanding the witnessing pattern of the classic phrase. Here, a tension exists between father language being normative and good, but mother language being possible and permissible.

Second, it is worth asking: can people "name" God? While Yahweh is the proper name of God and Jesus uses the term of endearment "Abba," this does not mean all attempts to use alternative language are subjective preferential assertions or projections. This is seen in the use of the word "trinity" itself. "Trinity," it should be noted, is not a word found in the Bible. It is the innovation proposed first by Tertullian, who also suggested a "three persons and one being" vocabulary that later thinkers further developed. This vocabulary is also not explicitly mentioned in the Bible, along with other terms of creedal orthodoxy. Biblicist Christians have struggled with this, but if the term trinity is acceptable and used in Christian worship to identify God, this speaks of the possibility of extra-biblical description that, while not literally stated in the text, has the capacity to encapsulate the whole meaning of the biblical message in a single term. Thus, the term trinity is an essential grammar for reading the biblical narrative properly. In worship, churches sing, "Blessed Trinity," and it seems that the designation of "Trinity" is able to offer a name-like title that describes accurately what God has revealed, despite it being a post-biblical description. Therefore, if this is true, in encountering God and being invited to respond, there is a kind of doxological capacity to further name God in ways that coincide with biblical revelation. Female experience is then, in conversation with God, able to suggest further names. Perhaps one of the earliest and most beautiful examples of this is when God rescues Hagar after Abraham casted her out. Genesis reports that she names the Lord who spoke with her *El-roi*, which means "The One Who Sees" (Gen 16:13). If what Hagar has done is legitimate, this suggests that believers are able to view the acts of God and are permitted to form names of God that praise God if they are congruent with canonical revelation. While father language is normative in function for many, it need not be viewed as exclusive.

Perhaps a third insight brings home this triune application of naming. As Augustine showed, the trinitarian relationships speak of God's essential identity as love. Augustine interpreted the trinitarian relationships as displaying God as lover, beloved, and the gift of love itself.[74] God is agapeic love. Not that love is God, but that agapeic love bears witness to God's character shown in the cross of Christ. To further the analogical way of speaking of God, where there is agapeic action, its goodness is from and participates in God's agapeic goodness. One thinks of Robert

---

74. Augustine, *The Trinity*, 8:5:10, 14.

Munch's book, *Love You Forever*, as a beautiful illustration that preachers are free to use in sermons coinciding with the metaphorical grammars previously spelled out. The mother says to her child, "I love you forever. I'll like you for always. As long as I am living my baby you'll be."[75] As moments of forgiveness and self-giving are moments where one's cross is taken-up and one embodies Christ, so also moments of motherly love speak of the being of God.

One touching example is worth mentioning. On January 7, 2015, Katherine Benefiel died in a housefire. Firefighters pulled her body out to find that she died shielding her five-year-old son from the flames.[76] She died protecting her child. Does not God love like this? Is not this love capable of illustrating what God does in Christ? Both the fatherly love and the motherly love that sacrifices for one's children speaks of the entire being of God, naming the action of all members of the Trinity, not just one. So, "Mother" need not be a title that replaces Father in the classic baptismal formula or Lord's Prayer—if they are understood in their counter-patriarchal intention—but "Mother" can be a way of identifying the love characteristic of each member and their whole being. This is the approach of Julian of Norwich (d. 1416) who famously referred to Christ as her Mother while not trying to revise his maleness: "he is our Mother."[77] She also applied motherhood to the whole Trinity: "the high might of the Trinity is our Father, and the deep wisdom of the Trinity is our Mother, and the great love of the Trinity is our Lord."[78] She refers to the entirety of the Trinity as having the properties of fatherliness, motherliness, and lordship, while referring to Jesus as "Mother Christ." Similarly, the theologian Joseph Jones has proposed the benediction: "God the Father, Son, and Holy Spirit, One God, Mother of us all."[79]

---

75. Munch, *Love You Forever*, [n.p.].
76. Sadly, the son died later due to his injuries, but that should not take away from the beauty of her own action. "Child Injured in Apt. Fire Dies."
77. Julian of Norwich, *Showings*, ch. 58.
78. Julian of Norwich, *Showings*, ch. 58.
79. Jones, *Grammar of Christian Faith*, 165.

Therefore, the trinitarian grammar qualifies the meaning of "Father" as a triune reference, but in turn, the term "Trinity" actually offers a pathway of naming God in ways that capture God's characteristics as the one revealed in the Gospel narrative, particularly seeing agapeic love as witness and therefore resource for referring to the Triune God.

Pneumatological

The last grammar might be called pneumatic, coinciding with the imminence of the Spirit in creation and God's inbreaking kingdom. The Spirit of God as the basis of life, the wisdom that fashioned creation with the first member of the Trinity, reiterates that all that is good in creation finds its source in God's goodness, but also further, the Spirit prophetically challenges idolatrous reductions of God to the creation, equipping the church for liberation. Speech of God must be life-affirming and liberating if it conforms to the Spirit.

Here again, there are characteristic misunderstandings in both conservative and feminist estimates. There is a conservative tendency to dismiss feminine language for the Spirit as unrealistic, particularly as it pertains to Lady Wisdom.[80] There is also a refusal to see gendered experience as a basis of theological reflection. Elizabeth Morelli writes,

> . . . insofar as we understand our access to God to be the very ground or core of the human spirit, then we cannot attribute to woman *qua* woman a specific conscious access to God. To do so would be to assert that woman is not quite human, or that there are two distinct human natures.[81]

Furthermore, there is a refusal to see pragmatic usages as offering the capacity to assess the meaning of convictions.[82] Meanwhile, the feminist priority of experience and liberation over and

---

80. Fyre, "Language for God," 36.
81. Morelli, "The Question of Woman's Experience," 236.
82. Molnar, *Divine Freedom*, 9. Molnar's criticism of Johnson is that she appeals overly to functional language, thus causing "desired social outcomes" to set the standard for God. This is frankly a caricature of Johnson's argument.

against revelation has unintended consequences. Strict appeals to human experience, whether feminine experience or human liberation as generalized categories, are challenged with the apparent plurality and ambiguity regarding what these mean if un-legitimated by realistic revelation. This is because language and symbols are malleable in how they are employed. Thus, general usage does not offer any clear guarantee that it will aid in liberating forms of life.[83] Religions with strong goddess figures are not necessarily less patriarchal.[84] Also, as Pamela Dickey Young notes, "there must be something normative in Christian identity and tradition prior to practice for a liberating practice to be normative. If not, others can preferentially claim their own practices as 'Christian' because principled criteria would have collapsed."[85] All experience is interpreted experience, and within patriarchal discourses, there are various ad hoc rationales and polemics employed where at times female voices can even be the defenders of patriarchal convictions. If a certain hierarchical social order is seen as proscribed by God and viewed as essential to trusting in God and God's authority, of course, questioning it does not seem at face value an attempt to be liberating. Thus, experience and liberation can be pliable categories and need further clarifications in particular forms of life and narratives of reference. Therefore, several clarifications are needed.

First, as the Spirit is the Spirit of life, coinciding with the previous analogical, metaphorical, and incarnational grammars, all of life *qua* life speaks of God. The Spirit is the source of order in creation (Gen 1:1–2). The Spirit is what renders life alive (Gen 2:7; Job 33:4; Ps 33:6). As Paul proclaims to the Athenians, in an astounding example, they are actually worshipping God through the altar to an unknown God (Acts 17:23). "For in him, we live and move and have our being" (Acts 17:28). This is a fascinating

83. So warns LaCugna, "God in Communion," 107.
84. Note, as Hanson argues, that while the religion of Israel by today's standards is quite patriarchal and regressive towards women, it was quite progressive in its own day against religions with more feminine depictions of deity, such as Babylonian and Philistine religion. Hanson, "Masculine Metaphors for God," 318.
85. Young, *Feminist Theology/Christian Theology*, 77.

instance as Paul quotes pagan poets, whose cultural conclusion about God being the Father over all, with all humanity as his offspring, becomes the basis by which the Gospel of Jesus Christ is introduced and repentance preached. As the Spirit is the basis of all goodness and being, wherever these are found, it is possible to speak about God alongside of them because they are understood to point to faith in Jesus Christ.[86] Note, then, that there is a kind of aporia: while all life speaks of God, this is really only truly seen as life through God. Just as narrative and name become mutually clarifying, so also works of creation and the descriptions of the Creator become mutually enriching. To affirm this possibility can be profoundly dignifying in a way that men, who have always heard male language, can fail to appreciate.[87]

Second, the imminence of God's creative activity is personified in the character of Lady Wisdom, which forms a viable way God reveals femininity. If Lady Wisdom in Proverbs is a pre-figure of the Holy Spirit, hypostasized wisdom is described as a "she" (Prov 1–9, but particularly 8:22–36). Many are content to dismiss Lady Wisdom as a personification, but given how strong the description of her is in the intertestamental literature such as the Wisdom of Solomon, where she is described as sharing in the divine prerogatives, this dismissal is not warranted. "She is a breath of the power of God, and a pure emanation of the glory of the Almighty" (Wis 7:25). "Although she is but One, she can do all things" (Wis 7:27). Wisdom is described as next to God at the

---

86. This is methodologically explicated in Moltmann, *Spirit of Life*, 17–39. "Anyone that stylizes revelation and experience into alternatives, ends up with revelations that cannot be experienced and experiences without revelation" (7). He goes on to say that God is the condition of all experience through the Spirit, and thus, properly understood through Christ, God is "in, with, and beneath" the experiences of everyday life (34).

87. Boulais-Duong, "The Power of a Pronoun" (blog), October 8, 2019. "I felt all the breath go out of my lungs and tears brim in my eyes. Only once before had I publicly heard the Christian God being referred to with a feminine pronoun. Then, just as it was that gray Sunday morning, the experience was powerful . . . I began using 'she' for God in my private prayers and journals. At times, I called her 'mother.' Using the feminine pronoun for God helped me to feel seen, valued, and affirmed in a way that I hadn't experienced yet as a woman in ministry."

throne and they together formed humanity (Wis 9:2–4). She is described in chs. 10–12 as doing all the actions of God in protecting the patriarchs, ransoming Israel out of Egypt, bringing them into the promise land, granting salvation to the righteous, and punishing the wicked. Lady Wisdom is identified as the Holy Spirit in Wis 7:7 ("I called on God and the Spirit of Wisdom came to me") and 9:17 ("Who has learned your counsel, unless you have given wisdom and sent your Holy Spirit from on high?"). If the deuterocanonical wisdom literature is at all illuminative of what Proverbs is speaking about,[88] then it is definitive: one member of the Trinity is identifiably female, and, according to the grammar of trinitarian attributes, what one has the others participate in as well. Athanasius suggested, an attribute that one has as deity, the other must also have as well, all except to say that they are the same person.[89] As Augustine argued, what one member does in history, all do eternally.[90] If God not only has Spirit but is Spirit,[91] and the Spirit is identified as a "she" in the Lady Wisdom prefigures, then this is a viable way to refer to God's entire being.[92] While the Spirit is the "Spirit of Christ" in the New Testament, the actions of the Spirit retain these motherly qualities.[93] Most notably, Matt 11:19 states that "Wisdom is known by her deeds," which may be referring to the Holy Spirit as Lady Wisdom acting in Christ. Whether or not this is metaphorical, "her" is used as a viable pronoun for referring to the Holy Spirit as the "Spirit of Wisdom" (Eph 1:17). This invalidates any strict attempt to argue that the Lady Wisdom language

88. Other references: Sir 24; Wis 6–9; Bar 3–4; 1 En. 42; 2 En. 30.
89. Athanasius, *Four Discourses*, 3:4.
90. Augustine, *The Trinity*, 1:2:4; 7. "Just as Father, Son, and Spirit are inseparable, so do they work inseparably." The more technical parsing is that what each member does "ad extra" that is individually in history, the one God does "ad intra," within God's eternal being.
91. This is the approach of Pinnock, *Flame of Love*, 15, 24–32.
92. This is developed by Johnson, *She Who Is*, 86–87.
93. For example, John 3:8 speaks of being "born again" by the Spirit. It may be argued that the dove of Jesus's baptism (e.g., Luke 3:22) is an allusion to the action of the Spirit "hovering" over the waters of creation (Gen 1:2) along with other allusions to a mother bird (Deut 32:11–12; Ps 57:1). Similarly, Jesus and Paul use the mother bird imagery (Matt 23:37–38; 1 Thess 2:7).

categorically ceases in the New Testament. Moreover, there is substantial evidence that the Spirit was worshipped in ancient Christianity as the "Mother of Christ."[94] To worship God "in Spirit" more than permits female usages based on the Old Testament pre-figures and early church examples. The early church did not see Father language so exclusive as to refuse others alongside of it.

Third, Christian faith purports that if God is God there is no domain of reality, and thus human experience, that is extraneous or meaningless to the creator of it and the Spirit of life. Thus, the question regarding experience as a source for Christian theology

---

94. van Oort, "The Holy Spirit as Feminine." Notable examples he cites include Origen, who states, "For if he who does the will of the Father in heaven is Christ's brother and sister and mother, and if the name of brother of Christ may be applied, not only to the race of men, but to beings of diviner rank than they, then there is nothing absurd in the Holy Spirit's being His Mother" (*Comm. Jo.* 2:6). Jerome concurs, both Origen and Jerome seem to be commentating on a passage from the lost Gospel to the Hebrews, but then looking to other biblical passages noting the femininity of the Spirit: "And also this: (in the text) 'like the eyes of a maid look to the hand of her mistress' (Ps 123:2), the maid is the soul and the mistress is the Holy Spirit. For also in that Gospel written according to the Hebrews, which the Nazoreans read, the Lord says: 'Just now, my Mother, the Holy Spirit, took me.' Nobody should be offended by this, for among the Hebrews the Spirit is said to be of the feminine gender although in our language it is called to be of masculine gender and in the Greek language neuter" (*Comm. Isa.* 11:40:9). Ephiphanius who states, "Next he describes Christ as a kind of power and also gives His dimensions . . . And the Holy Spirit is (said to be) like Christ, too, but She is a female being" (*Pan.* 19:4:1–2). Hippolytus who says similarly, "There should also be a female with Him (i.e., with Christ as an angel) . . . The male is the Son of God and the female is called the Holy Spirit" (*Haer.* 9:13:3). Melito of Sardis has a prayer invoking worship that reads as follows: "Hymn the Father, you holy ones; sing to your Mother, virgins" (Frag. 17). In discussing chastity before marriage, Aphrahat states, "As long as a man has not taken a wife he loves and reveres God his Father and the Holy Spirit his Mother, and he has no other love" (*Dem.* 18). Aphrahat then describes the work of the Spirit in baptism as that of a female dove: "From baptism we receive the Spirit of Christ, and in the same hour that the priests invoke the Spirit, she opens the heavens and descends, and hovers over the waters (cf. Gen 1:2), and those who are baptized put Her on" (*Dem.* 6). These examples are enough to warrant that the ancient church did at times include mother and father language in its theology and worship.

should not be whether but how. The biblical narrative and core Christian convictions open Christian theology up to experience and experience to conviction. The revelation of all humanity in the image of God, the kingdom of God where the lowly are raised up, the saving of all flesh in the incarnation of Christ, the Spirit being poured out on all flesh, a community that calls to listen and discern, etc., are all criterial resources that are authentically Christian and biblical by which female voices (or any that can be identified as victimized, oppressed, abused, etc.) can and must become normative for Christian faithfulness. Thus, incorporating other voices results in undoing the ways patriarchal discourses have suppressed not only women today, but even the full content of Christian history and its Scriptures. Pamela Dickey Young offers good nuance in this regard in stating that "women's experience" means several things: (1) Women's bodies as different from men's; (2) Women's social experience where submission of women is emphasized and sexual appeal to men is emphasized; (3) Women have experience of direct oppression based on gender; (4) Women's historical experience is often "lost" and in need of recovery; and (5) women's experience can thus be the catalyst for social change.[95]

Fourth, to go further, this pneumatic aspect of thinking about God shows that imminence of the Spirit is the presence of liberation, such that the feminist pragmatic criterion, when understood through the biblical narrative (not despite it), is valid. A few examples illustrate this: Isa 61:1–3 indicates that the Spirit will come upon the anointed messiah (which Jesus claims for his own in Luke 4:18–19) and that his message is one of "good news to the oppressed," "binding up the broken hearted," "freedom to the captives," and "release of the prisoners." Meanwhile, Jesus, echoing the prophets, warned that "they honor me with their lips, but their hearts are far from me" (Matt 15:8). Mere assent to certain language cannot demonstrate true sincerity or purity of belief. Only action shows this. As Paul identifies the gift of the Spirit upon all people regardless of bias, so also the gifts of the Spirit are bestowed in coinciding fashion (Gal 3:28; 1 Cor

95. Young, *Feminist Theology/Christian Theology*, 53–56.

12:13). If Gentiles are justified by the Spirit, then women are also gifted to lead the church by this same unprejudiced Spirit. This forms an important rule: "where the Spirit is, there is freedom" (2 Cor 3:17). This is not dualistic, spiritualized inner freedom nor is it the liberal obsession with autonomy apart from morality, but rather, material liberty to respond to God's call. Scripture itself then permits a means by which its language can be criticized if it is being used against its own liberating intention. In Matthew, Christ instructs that teachers are known (and therefore their teaching is assessed) by their fruit (Matt 7:17). Paul similarly seems to, in part, reject circumcision despite its theological import in the Old Testament because it was being used to foster ethnic superiority. For Paul, circumcision does not fulfill its purpose, where only "faith expressing itself through love" (Gal 5:6) counts; in other words, actions that produce the fruit of the Spirit, "against such things there are no law" (Gal 5:23). The Spirit is seen in the effects of convictions, and the Spirit can then judge between what words are dead letters or living words.

This permits the final aspect of pneumatic grammar: the potential for prophetic and iconoclastic revisions. Rabbi Abraham Joshua Heschel once said that "The prophet is an iconoclast, challenging the apparently holy, revered, and awesome. Beliefs cherished as certainties, instructions endowed with supreme sanctity, he [or she—did Heschel forget about Deborah and Huldah?] exposes as scandalous pretension."[96] While the theology and practices of the temple were instituted by none other than Moses, essential to understanding the presence of God with the people, the prophets' message overtly negated and contradicted these institutes as they were used to foster apathy, arrogance, and neglect of justice. In the face of the promises of God to protect and be with the people, they proclaimed prophetic messages such as the message of Hosea: "You are not my people and I am not your God" (Hos 1:9). They did not hesitate to negate convictions central to Israel's revealed testimony, whether affirmations of God's character, God's promises, the laws, and the temple, when

---

96. Heschel, *The Prophets*, 1:10.

their function caused the neglect of sincerity, humility, justice, and righteousness. Similarly, Jesus continued these prophetic critiques of the temple sacrifices and purity laws. Jesus's use of "Abba" brings an intimacy to God language where the Pharisees stressed distance, countering how their convictions functioned. Scripture does permit the reflection and revision of symbols and images in light of their intended purposes. If God can be Father but not Mother, moreover, if it functions to prioritize the male over the female, that might be a good indication that God has been reduced to a thing.[97] The accusation that this can be "idolatrous" is harsh but accurate. If father language is used to overtly or implicitly reinforce patriarchy, the necessity of prophetic iconoclasm is apparent, just as the temple needed to have its tables turned. God's transcendence is given realistically in imminence, but these do not mean it can be grasped so as to be taken for granted. Prophetic discourse, as Ricoeur notes, inherently "reorients by first disorienting," through hyperboles and iconoclastic negations.[98] However, there is always a challenge. For example, praying the "Our Mother" gives the impression that biblical revelation is being subverted by human assertion (as the concerns of the earlier grammars have shown), and thus doing so may be counterproductive in some congregations. However, the notion that language cannot be negated with others in a kind of prophetic or iconoclastic mode fails to realize that this is permitted in how the Bible uses its own language with other terms. It is not whether it can be permitted, it is whether the congregation has been taught to listen to hear it for what it is.[99] Where the grammar is not understood, the words are unintelligible. The question then becomes, have many churches failed to cultivate the listening practices necessary to be open to prophetic voices? The notion that an iconoclastic revision cannot happen may be the very reason why it should.

---

97. McFague, *Metaphorical Theology*, 190.
98. Ricoeur, "Naming God," 229.
99. See Chilton and Harmon, "Conclusion," 293–308.

Thus, the pneumatological adds the final grammar that brings this investigation full circle. The Spirit's imminence in creation allows for the goodness of creation *qua* creation and the human *qua* human to offer data to reflect on God. Rather than being independent of revelation or the Bible filtering these sources, the Bible should be understood to aid in equipping the person to listen to these sources rightly, or else experience is prone to ambiguity. When this is done, the Bible puts forward liberation of the marginalized as a valid criterion for evaluation, fostering the possibility of prophetic and iconoclastic discourses and actions that are in keeping with how the Prophets and Jesus handled their own religious heritage.

Conclusion

Thus, in determining gendered language for God, certain grammars need to be upheld: (1) language cannot neglect to articulate itself in a way that upholds realistic revelation (and it is in a deeper understanding of revelation that simple proof-texts are rendered problematic); (2) language does not speak in a literalistic way, reducing God to the created order or failing to uphold divine transcendence and ineffability; (3) language is problematic if it refuses the goodness of creation that all speaks of God in analogical and metaphorical ways; (4) language must pattern itself based on the narratives of God's works and it cannot be out of congruence with the narratives of the life of Jesus Christ, his death, and resurrection; (5) language cannot refuse a Triune structure of agapeic love; and finally, (6) language must be in agreement with the prophetic and liberating imminence of the Spirit, Lady Wisdom. These grammars are not posited as separate rules, but rather each works in conjunction with the others.

Readers of this essay may find it frustrating in the way that essays attempting a middle-ground, mediating view can be. This essay may be one man's critique of feminist theology alongside of more nuanced feminists and a critique of conservative theology through the appropriation of voices from the tradition. Conservatives will undoubtably notice that liturgical revision is regarded here as more than permissible since the claim that

"Father" is a proper name does not hold water, much less the notion that the Bible does not contain direct references and implicit logic by which God can be considered feminine and a mother. This essay has demonstrated this on multiple fronts. Conservatives fear that the loss of the title Father de-particularizes the divine identity. However, given Scripture's own diversity on the matter, and the fact that particularization happens through the whole of the narrative with all of its language holistically, not by just one word, this is simply not the case. Meanwhile, some feminists may dislike the conclusion that not all father language is patriarchal,[100] and in fact, that it can be intended to counter patriarchy. Furthermore, some may not like that the experience of women (or the category of "liberation") is not so uniform and clear as some would purport it to be to legitimate a revisionist agenda. Yet, this contextual aspect of grammar means that this conclusion eludes simple proscriptions. This is important to stress because talk of experience often gives the impression that men prefer father language and women prefer mother language, that liturgical language should be revised to have a neat 50/50 split in the references, or that mother language is always the solution to curb patriarchy in all contexts. Jürgen Moltmann has written on why feminism liberates men from patriarchy as well,

---

100. Biggs, "Gender and God-Talk," 15–25. Biggs provides clear and nuanced work, offering a similar grammatical reflection as this essay (although he does not call it that). He shows the contexts of Father language in the midst of paganism and how Father language moves from being analogical to self-defining, and thus makes a case for its enduring importance: "God is revealed using 'Father' language in Scripture in a way that 'Mother' language never reveals God in Scripture" (23). However, he admits, ". . . both are coherent and respectable positions which take account of how language works and what the biblical evidence is, and which take the Bible seriously in Christian life and thinking . . . My own practice encapsulates my ability to defend both sides of the matter: I continue to pray to God as Father, but believe that God would not in fact mind if I did otherwise. If those of both opinions were equally at ease with each other in this matter then perhaps that would be appropriate to the complexity of sorting out the question of gender and God-talk" (24).

which must be emphasized.[101] Meanwhile, Janet Martin Soskice has written on how feminists can productively employ father language.[102] Usage is more complex than simple solutions. While there are versions of feminism that undermine revealed realism and versions of conservatism that are prone to literalization, what this essay argues is that just as traditional language is not by intention sexist, so too there is liberty to use mother references.[103] To some extent, the intent of this essay is to show that those that are concerned about the authority of revelation and those that are concerned about the liberation of women ought not to be so opposed. When the grammar of revelation is understood, a liberty of usages, that are in turn liberating, becomes possible and, in many ways, necessary. When the grammar of liberation is understood, deep regard for biblically normed discourse is necessary. Liberation renders revelation faithfully, while revelation renders liberation intelligibly.[104]

---

101. Moltmann, *Experiences in Theology*. His chapter "Feminist Theology for Men" (268–93) is a good argument for why feminism is not just beneficial to women.

102. See Soskice, "Can a Feminist?" 94. "Does the 'father God' have a future? If Christianity has a future, then the answer is probably 'yes.'"

103. For an excellent pastoral resource, see Smith, *Is It Okay to Call God "Mother?"* It is a rich yet easy to understand resource for a church board or Bible study group.

104. LaCugna concludes something similar in "God in Communion," 107: "If the Christian community were truly to become that which it is destined to become, namely, the community of all persons who have realized their common vocation to praise and glorify God and to be united in service to others, then the question whether to call God Mother or Father would take on a different significance. In a true community of stewards, where orthopraxis (practice of truth) would finally have coincided with orthodoxy (right opinion about the mystery of salvation), the whole range of human experience would be incorporated into our praise with God. This is where the trinitarian and Christian feminist agenda intersect. In the current controversy it is essential to keep in mind that all of us are united in the common desire to praise God."

Bibliography

Achtemeier, Elizabeth. "Exchanging God for 'No gods': A Discussion of Female Language for God." In *Speaking the Christian God: The Holy Trinity and the Challenges of Feminism*, edited by Alvin F. Kimel, Jr., 1–16. Grand Rapids: Eerdmans, 1992.

Anderson, Ray. "The Incarnation of God in Feminist Christology: A Theological Critique." In *Speaking the Christian God: The Holy Trinity and the Challenges of Feminism*, edited by Alvin F. Kimel, Jr., 288–312. Grand Rapids: Eerdmans, 1992.

Anselm of Canterbury. *The Prayers and Meditations of Saint Anselm with the Proslogion*. Translated by Sister Benedicta Ward. New York: Penguin, 1997.

Aquinas, Thomas. *Summa Contra Gentiles*. Translated by Anton Pegis. Notre Dame: University of Notre Dame Press, 1955.

Athanasius. *Four Discourses Against the Arians*. In *Athanasius, Selected Works and Letters*. Vol. 4 of *The Nicene and Post-Nicene Fathers of the Christian Church*. Grand Rapids: Eerdmans, 1971.

Augustine. *The Trinity*. Translated by Edmund Hill. 2nd ed. New York: New York City Press, 2015.

Biale, David. "The God with Breasts: El Shaddai in the Bible." *History of Religions* 21 (1982) 240–56.

Biggs, Richard. "Gender and God-Talk: Can We Call God 'Mother'?" *Themelios* 29 (2004) 15–25.

Bloesch, Donald. *Battle for the Trinity*. Ann Arbor, MI: Vine Books, 1985.

———. *Is the Bible Sexist?* Eugene, OR: Wipf & Stock, 2001.

———. *A Theology of Word and Spirit: Authority and Method in Theology.* Exeter: Paternoster, 1992.

Boulais-Duong, Lindsey. "The Power of a Pronoun: How What We Call God Affects Everything." *Mutuality*, October 8, 2019, https://www.cbeinternational.org/resource/article/mutuality-blog-magazine/power-pronoun-how-what-we-call-god-affects-everything

Brueggemann, Walter. *Old Testament Theology.* Minneapolis: Fortress, 1997.

Bynum, Caroline Walker. *Jesus as Mother: Studies in the Spirituality of the High Middle Ages.* Berkeley: University of California Press, 1982.

Carr, Anne. *Transforming Grace.* San Francisco: Harper & Row, 1988.

"Child Injured in Harrison Apt. Fire Dies." KLRT-Fox16. January 15, 2015. https://www.fox16.com/news/child-injured-in-harrison-apt-fire-dies/.

Chilton, Amy, and Steven Harmon. "Conclusion: Light from Converted Listening." In *Sources of Light: Resources for Baptist Churches Practicing Theology*, edited by Amy Chilton and Steven Harmon, 293–308. Macon, GA: Mercer University Press, 2020.

Chrysostom, John. *Homilies on the Gospel of Saint Matthew.* Vol. 10 of *The Nicene and Post Nicene Fathers.* Grand Rapids: Eerdmans Publishing, 1956.

Clement of Alexandria. *Christ the Educator.* Translated by Simon Wood. Fathers of the Church 23. Washington, DC: Catholic University of America Press, 1954.

———. *Who is the Rich Man that Shall Be Saved?* Translated by G. W. Butterworth. Cambridge, MA: Harvard University Press, 1953.

Cooper, John. *Our Father in Heaven: Christian Faith and Inclusive Language for God.* Grand Rapids: Baker, 1998.

Daly, Mary. *Beyond God the Father: Towards a Philosophy of Women's Liberation.* Boston: Beacon, 1973.

"Declaration *Inter Insigniores* on the Question of Admission of Women to the Ministerial Priesthood." *Sacred Congregation for the Doctrine of the Faith.* October 15, 1976. Online: https://www.vatican.va/roman_curia/congregations/cfaith/documents/rc_con_cfaith_doc_19761015_inter-insigniores_en.html

Dionysius. *Pseudo-Dionysius: The Complete Works.* Translated by Colm Luibheid. New York: Paulist, 1987.

Frei, Hans. *The Identity of Jesus Christ.* Eugene, OR: Wipf & Stock, 1997.

Fyre, Roland Mushat. "Language for God and Feminist Language: Problems and Principles." In *Speaking the Christian God: The Holy Trinity and the Challenges of Feminism,* edited by Alvin F. Kimel, Jr., 17–43. Grand Rapids: Eerdmans, 1992.

Geffe, Claude. "'Father' as the Proper Name of God." In *God as Father?,* edited by Johannes-Baptist Metz and Edward Schillebeeckx, 43–50. New York: Seabury, 1981.

Grenz, Stanley. *The Named God and the Question of Being.* Louisville: Westminster John Knox, 2005.

Grudem, Wayne, and John Piper, eds. *Recovering Biblical Manhood and Womanhood: A Response to Evangelical Feminism*. Wheaton, IL: Crossway, 2012.

Gunton, Colin. "Proteus and Procrustes: A Study in the Dialectic of Language in Disagreement with Sallie McFague." In *Speaking the Christian God: The Holy Trinity and the Challenges of Feminism*, edited by Alvin F. Kimel, Jr., 65–80. Grand Rapids: Eerdmans, 1992.

Haddad, Mimi. "Evidence for and Significance of Feminine God Language from the Church Fathers to the Modern Era." *Priscilla Papers* (July 2004). No pages. Online: https://www.cbeinternational.org/resource/article/priscilla-papers-academic-journal/evidence-and-significance-feminine-god-language?page=5.

Hamerton-Kelly, Robert. *God the Father: Theology and Patriarchy in the Teachings of Jesus*. Minneapolis: Fortress, 1979.

Hanson, Paul. "Masculine Metaphors for God and Sex-discrimination in the Old Testament." *Ecumenical Review* 27 (1975) 316–24.

Heschel, Abraham Joshua. *The Prophets*. 2 vols. New York: Harper & Row, 1962.

Jewett, Paul. *God, Creation, and Revelation: A Neo-Evangelical Theology*. Grand Rapids: Eerdmans, 1991.

Johnson, Elizabeth. *Consider Jesus*. New York: Crossroads, 1990.

———. "Redeeming the Name of Christ: Christology." In *Freeing Theology: The Essentials of Theology in Feminist Perspective*, edited by Catherine Mowry LaCugna, 115–27. New York: Harper Collins, 1993.

———. *She Who Is*. New York: Crossroad, 1993.

Johnson, Luke Timothy. *The Real Jesus*. New York: HarperCollins, 1996.

Jones, Joseph. *Grammar of Christian Faith*. Lanham, MD: Rowman & Littlefield, 2002.

Julian of Norwich. *Showings*. Translated by Edmund Colledge. New York: Paulist, 1978.

Kimel Jr., Alvin F. "The God who Likes His Name: Holy Trinity, Feminism, and the Language of Faith." In *Speaking the Christian God: The Holy Trinity and the Challenges of Feminism*, edited by Alvin F. Kimel Jr., 188–208. Grand Rapids: Eerdmans, 1992.

Kimel Jr., Alvin F., ed. *Speaking the Christian God: The Holy Trinity and the Challenges of Feminism*. Grand Rapids: Eerdmans, 1992.

LaCugna, Catherine Mowry. "The Baptismal Formula, Feminist Objections, and Trinitarian Theology." *Journal of Ecumenical Studies* 26 (1989) 235–50.

———. "God in Communion with Us: The Trinity." In *Freeing Theology: The Essentials of Theology in Feminist Perspective*, edited by Catherine Mowry LaCugna, 83–114. New York: HarperCollins, 1993.

LaCugna, Catherine Mowry, ed. *Freeing Theology: The Essentials of Theology in Feminist Perspective*. New York: HarperCollins, 1993.

Lindbeck, George. *Nature of Doctrine: Religion and Theology in a Postliberal Age*. Louisville: Westminster John Knox, 1984.

Long, D. Stephen. *Speaking of God*. Grand Rapids: Eerdmans, 2009.

Matthis, David. "Why Jesus Was Not A Woman." *Desiring God* (October 2020). No pages. Online: https://www.desiringgod.org/articles/why-jesus-was-not-a-woman.

McFague, Sallie. *The Body of God*. Minneapolis: Fortress, 1993.

———. *Metaphorical Theology*. Philadelphia: Fortress, 1982.

———. *Models of God*. Minneapolis: Fortress, 1988.

McGregor-Wright, R. K. "God, Metaphor, and Gender: Is the God of the Bible a Male Deity?" In *Discovering Biblical Equality: Complementarity without Hierarchy*, edited by Ronald Pierce and Rebecca Merrill Groothuis, 287–301. Downers Grove, IL: IVP Academic, 2005.

Mollenkott, Virginia Ramsey. *The Divine Feminine: The Biblical Imagery of God as Female*. Eugene, OR: Wipf & Stock, 1987.

Molnar, Paul. *Divine Freedom and the Doctrine of the Immanent Trinity*. London: T. & T. Clark, 2002.

Moltmann, Jurgen. *Experiences in Theology*. Translated by Margaret Kohl. Minneapolis: Fortress, 2000.

———. "The Fatherly Mother: Is Trinitarian Patripassianism Replacing Theological Patriarchalism?" In *God as Father?*, edited by Johannes-Baptist Metz and Edward Schillebeeckx, 51–56. New York: Seabury, 1981.

———. *Spirit of Life*. Translated by Margaret Kohl. Minneapolis: Fortress, 2001.

Morelli, Elizabeth A. "The Question of Woman's Experience of God." In *Speaking the Christian God: The Holy Trinity and the Challenges of Feminism*, edited by Alvin F. Kimel, Jr., 222–36. Grand Rapids: Eerdmans, 1992.

Munch, Robert. *Love You Forever*. Toronto: Firefly, 1986.

Packer, J. I. *Knowing God*. Downers Grove, IL: InterVarsity, 1973.

Pannenberg, Wolfhart. *Systematic Theology*. 3 vols. Translated by Geoffrey Bromiley. Grand Rapids: Eerdmans, 1997.

Pinnock, Clark. *Flame of Love*. Downers Grove, IL: InterVarsity Press, 1996.

Powell, Mark Allan. *Jesus as a Figure in History*. 2nd ed. Louisville: Westminster John Knox, 2013.

"Resolution on God the Father." Online: https://www.sbc.net/resource-library/resolutions/resolution-on-god-the-father/

Ricoeur, Paul. "Fatherhood: From Phantasm to Symbol." In *The Conflict of Interpretations: Essays in Hermeneutics*, edited by Don Ihde, 468–98. Evanston, IL: Northwestern University Press, 1974.

———. "Naming God." In *Figuring the Sacred: Religion, Narrative, and Imagination*, edited by Richard Kearney, 217–35. Minneapolis: Augsburg Press, 1995.

———. *The Rule of Metaphor: Multi-Disciplinary Studies in the Creation of Meaning in Language*. Toronto: University of Toronto Press, 1978.

Ruether, Rosemary Radford. "The Liberation of Christology from Patriarchy." In *Feminist Theology: A Reader*, edited by Ann Loades, 138–47. London: SPCK, 1990.

―――. *Sexism and God-Talk*. Boston: Beacon, 1983.

Schneiders, Sandra. "The Bible and Feminism: Biblical Theology." In *Freeing Theology: The Essentials of Theology in Feminist Perspective*, edited by Catherine Mowry LaCugna, 31–57. New York: Harper Collins, 1993.

Smith, Paul. *Is it Okay to Call God "Mother?"* Peabody, MA: Hendrickson, 1993.

Soskice, Janet Martin. "Can a Feminist Call God 'Father'?" In *Speaking the Christian God: The Holy Trinity and the Challenges of Feminism*, edited by Alvin F. Kimel, Jr., 81–94. Grand Rapids: Eerdmans, 1992.

―――. *Metaphor and Religious Language*. Oxford: Clarendon Press, 1985.

Soulen, R. Kendall. "The Name of the Holy Trinity: A Triune Name." *Modern Theology* 59 (2002) 244–61.

Spencer, Aida. "Jesus' Treatment of Women in the Gospels." In *Discovering Biblical Equality: Complementarity without Hierarchy*, edited by Ronald Pierce and Rebecca Merrill Groothuis, 126–41. Downers Grove, IL: IVP Academic, 2005.

Teresa of Avila. *Interior Castle*. Translated by K. Kavanaugh and O. Rodriguez. New York: Paulist, 1979.

van Oort, Johannes. "The Holy Spirit as Feminine: Early Christian Testimonies and Their Interpretation." *Theological Studies* 72 (2016). No Pages. Online: https://hts.org.za/index.php/hts/article/view/3225/7763.

Visser't Hooft, W. A. *The Fatherhood of God in an Age of Emancipation*. Philadelphia: Westminster, 1982.

Webb, William. *Slaves, Women, and Homosexuals: Exploring the Hermeneutics of Transcultural Analysis.* Downers Grove, IL: InterVarsity, 2001.

Wittgenstein, Ludwig. *Philosophical Investigations.* Translated by G. E. Anscombe. Oxford: Blackwell, 1953.

Wright, G. Ernst. *God who Acts: Biblical Theology as Recital.* Naperville, IL: Alec Allenson, 1960.

Young, Pamela Dickey. *Feminist Theology/Christian Theology: In Search of Method.* Minneapolis: Fortress, 1990.

https://www.mcmaster.ca/mjtm/volume21.htm

Matthew W. Bates. *Gospel Allegiance: What Faith in Jesus Misses for Salvation in Christ.* Grand Rapids: Brazos, 2019. Reviewed by John J. H. Lee.

Richard P. Belcher Jr. *Finding Favour in the Sight of God: A Theology of Wisdom Literature.* New Studies in Biblical Theology 46. Downers Grove, IL: InterVarsity, 2018. Reviewed by Matthew Bovard.

Rowan Williams. *Christ the Heart of Creation.* New York: Bloomsbury Continuum, 2018. Reviewed by Spencer Miles Boersma.

Michael McClymond. *The Devil's Redemption: A New History and Interpretation of Christian Universalism.* 2 vols. Grand Rapids: Baker Academic, 2018. Reviewed by Spencer Miles Boersma.

Ilaria L. E. Ramelli. *Universal Salvation from Christian Beginnings to Julian of Norwich.* Vol. 1 of A Larger Hope? Eugene, OR: Cascade, 2019. Reviewed by Spencer Miles Boersma.

Robin A. Parry with Ilaria L. E. Ramelli. *Universal Salvation from the Reformation to the Nineteenth Century.* Vol. 2 of A Larger Hope? Eugene, OR: Cascade, 2019. Reviewed by Spencer Miles Boersma.

Eleonore Stump. *Atonement.* Oxford Studies in Analytic Theology. New York: Oxford University Press, 2018. Reviewed by Aaron Brian Davis.

Walter Brueggemann. *Virus as a Summons to Faith: Biblical Reflections in a Time of Loss, Grief, and Uncertainty.* Eugene, OR: Cascade, 2020. Reviewed by Chris S. Stevens.

Dennis Ngien, ed. *The Interface of Science, Theology, and Religion: Essays in Honor of Alister E. McGrath.* Eugene, OR: Pickwick, 2019. Reviewed by Gerhard Mielke.

Nijay K. Gupta. *Prepare, Succeed, Advance: A Guidebook for Getting a PhD in Biblical Studies and Beyond.* 2nd ed. Eugene, OR: Cascade, 2019. Reviewed by Dustin Burlet.

Mark Galli. *Karl Barth: An Introductory Biography for Evangelicals.* Grand Rapids: Eerdmans, 2017. Reviewed by Geoffrey Butler.

Justin Giboney et al. *Compassion (&) Conviction: The AND Campaign's Guide to Faithful Civic Engagement.* Downers Grove, IL: InterVarsity, 2020. Reviewed by Geoffrey Butler.

Chelle L. Stearns. *Handling Dissonance: A Musical Theological Aesthetic of Unity.* Eugene, OR: Pickwick, 2019. Reviewed by Bradley K. Broadhead.

David Rylaarsdam. *John Chrysostom on Divine Pedagogy: The Coherence of His Theology and Preaching.* Oxford Early Christian Studies. Oxford: Oxford University Press, 2014. Reviewed by Mark Hanson.

Nijay K. Gupta. *Paul and the Language of Faith.* Grand Rapids: Eerdmans, 2020. Reviewed by William B. Bowes.

Raphael Lataster. *Questioning the Historicity of Jesus: Why a Philosophical Analysis Elucidates the Historical Discourse.* Value Inquiry Book Series (Philosophy and Religion) 336. Leiden: Brill | Rodopi, 2019. Reviewed by Christopher M. Hansen.

www.ingramcontent.com/pod-product-compliance
Lightning Source LLC
Chambersburg PA
CBHW051941160426
43198CB00013B/2254